# Domestic Violence and Abuse

Editor: Tracy Biram

Volume 370

Loughborough College

LC060616

Inde                Publishers

First published by Independence Educational Publishers

The Studio, High Green

Great Shelford

Cambridge CB22 5EG

England

© Independence 2020

ISBN-13: 978 1 86168 827 9

## Printed in Great Britain

Zenith Print Group

# Contents

## Chapter 1: Facts and Statistics

Forms of domestic violence   1

What is coercive control?   2

Coercive control incidents double in a year, as campaigners warn domestic abuse 'remains at epidemic levels'   3

Domestic abuse in England and Wales overview: November 2019   4

Domestic abuse in Scotland: 2018-2019 statistics   6

Domestic abuse recorded by the police in Scotland, 2018-2019   7

Jess Phillips MP: The Domestic Abuse Bill is to be welcomed, but there is still work to be done   8

Challenging the myths   9

Statistics: Violence in Scotland   12

'A national travesty': Domestic abuse rises 24% as number of cases passed for charge falls 11%   13

Over half of UK women killed by men die at hands of partner or ex   15

Attacks on family members by women rise twice as fast as by men, new report shows   16

## Chapter 2: Victims of Abuse

Coronavirus lockdown is a dangerous time for victims of domestic abuse – here's what you need to know   17

Nearly 700 children identified as being at risk of domestic violence every day, figures show   18

Over 200,000 elderly people experienced domestic abuse in 2017/18   19

Shedding light on the dark side of teen dating: dating violence   20

Teenagers need to know where love stops and abusive relationships start   22

Are a third of domestic abuse victims men?   24

Male victims of domestic abuse face barriers to accessing support services – new study   26

Gravesham woman lost her home after partner was bailed out for domestic abuse   27

Domestic violence is widely accepted in most developing countries, new study reveals   28

## Chapter 3: Tackling Domestic Violence

Government publishes landmark domestic abuse bill   30

Enhanced domestic abuse bill introduced to Parliament   31

Domestic abuse bill not enough to save 'life-saving' services, campaigners warn   32

How to prevent abuse in teenage relationships   34

Relationship education could help reduce domestic violence   35

Worried about a friend?   36

'Domestic violence prevention course was no cure, but a salvation'   38

Key Facts   40

Glossary   41

Activities   42

Index   43

Acknowledgements   44

# Introduction

*Domestic Violence and Abuse* is Volume 370 in the **ISSUES** series. The aim of the series is to offer current, diverse information about important issues in our world, from a UK perspective.

## ABOUT DOMESTIC VIOLENCE AND ABUSE

According to the Office of National Statistics (ONS) about 4.2% of men and 8.4% of women suffered domestic abuse in England and Wales during 2019. Anyone can be a victim of domestic violence, regardless of gender, age, ethnicity, socio-economic status, sexuality or background. This book looks at different types of abuse, explores facts, statistics and myths surrounding the issue and considers different approaches to tackling this serious problem.

## OUR SOURCES

Titles in the **ISSUES** series are designed to function as educational resource books, providing a balanced overview of a specific subject.

The information in our books is comprised of facts, articles and opinions from many different sources, including:

◆ Newspaper reports and opinion pieces

◆ Website factsheets

◆ Magazine and journal articles

◆ Statistics and surveys

◆ Government reports

◆ Literature from special interest groups.

## A NOTE ON CRITICAL EVALUATION

Because the information reprinted here is from a number of different sources, readers should bear in mind the origin of the text and whether the source is likely to have a particular bias when presenting information (or when conducting their research). It is hoped that, as you read about the many aspects of the issues explored in this book, you will critically evaluate the information presented.

It is important that you decide whether you are being presented with facts or opinions. Does the writer give a biased or unbiased report? If an opinion is being expressed, do you agree with the writer? Is there potential bias to the 'facts' or statistics behind an article?

## ASSIGNMENTS

In the back of this book, you will find a selection of assignments designed to help you engage with the articles you have been reading and to explore your own opinions. Some tasks will take longer than others and there is a mixture of design, writing and research-based activities that you can complete alone or in a group.

## FURTHER RESEARCH

At the end of each article we have listed its source and a website that you can visit if you would like to conduct your own research. Please remember to critically evaluate any sources that you consult and consider whether the information you are viewing is accurate and unbiased.

# Useful websites

www.bristol.ac.uk

www.fullfact.org

www.gov.uk

www.independent.co.uk

www.kentonline.co.uk

www.loverespect.co.uk

www.news-decoder.com

www.ons.gov.uk

www.politicshome.com

www.refuge.org.uk

www.telegraph.co.uk

www.theconversation.com

www.weforum.org

www.womensaid.org.uk

www.zerotolerance.org.uk

# Forms of domestic abuse

**D**omestic violence is the abuse of one partner within an intimate or family relationship. It is the repeated, random and habitual use of intimidation to control a partner. The abuse can be physical, emotional, psychological, financial or sexual. Anyone forced to alter their behaviour because they are frightened of their partner's reaction is being abused.

Most people can identify physical abuse – it is the most 'obvious' form of domestic violence. But what about the more subtle forms? This page gives information on the other techniques perpetrators may use to abuse and control.

## Emotional abuse

Sometimes called 'psychological abuse', emotional abuse is an attack on a woman's personality rather than her body, and it can be just as harmful as physical abuse.

Examples include calling her names, putting her down, making her feel like she is going mad and blaming her for the abuse, or controlling her every move through threats and intimidation. The grinding impact of emotional abuse can chip away at a woman's sense of self. She may gradually begin to believe her abuser when he tells her, day in, day out, that she is worthless, that no-one will believe her, that no-one cares about her but him.

## Sexual abuse

Approximately 90% of those who are raped know the perpetrator prior to the offence. Sexual abuse – including rape, sexual assault and sexual exploitation – is commonly used by domestic violence perpetrators as a way to control and abuse their partners. Sexual abuse is any form of sexual activity (involving physical contact, words or photographs) that takes place without the other person's full and informed consent. It makes no difference whether a man's wife or girlfriend has consented in the past. Sexual abuse also includes an abuser withholding his partner's access to contraception, or forcing her into sexual practices she finds degrading.

## Financial abuse

Financial abuse – or economic abuse – is a way of controlling a person's ability to acquire, use and maintain their own money and resources. Financial abuse can take many forms. Abusers may prevent a woman from earning or accessing her own money (for example, by banning her from going out to work, or sabotaging job interviews, or by taking the welfare benefits she is entitled to); spend or take her money without consent; build up debts in her name; or damage her possessions or property. If a woman is separated from the abuser, he might withhold child maintenance payments.

*January 2020*

# What is coercive control?

Domestic abuse isn't always physical. Coercive control is an act or a pattern of acts of assault, threats, humiliation and intimidation or other abuse that is used to harm, punish or frighten their victim.

This controlling behaviour is designed to make a person dependent by isolating them from support, exploiting them, depriving them of independence and regulating their everyday behaviour.

We campaigned and succeeded in making coercive control a criminal offence. This has marked a huge step forward in tackling domestic abuse. But now we want to make sure that everyone understands what it is.

Coercive control creates invisible chains and a sense of fear that pervades all elements of a victim's life. It works to limit their human rights by depriving them of their liberty and reducing their ability for action. Experts like Evan Stark liken coercive control to being taken hostage. As he says: 'the victim becomes captive in an unreal world created by the abuser, entrapped in a world of confusion, contradiction and fear.'

## How do you know if this is happening to you?

Some common examples of coercive behaviour are:

- Isolating you from friends and family
- Depriving you of basic needs, such as food
- Monitoring your time
- Monitoring you via online communication tools or spyware
- Taking control over aspects of your everyday life, such as where you can go, who you can see, what you can wear and when you can sleep
- Depriving you of access to support services, such as medical services
- Repeatedly putting you down, such as saying you're worthless
- Humiliating, degrading or dehumanising you
- Controlling your finances
- Making threats or intimidating you.

## Statistics on coercive control

- The Crown Prosecution Service Case information system recorded 960 offences of coercive and controlling behaviour where a prosecution commenced at magistrates' courts in the year ending March 2018. This is a three-fold increase from 309 in the year ending March 2017 (ONS, 2018). 97% of defendants prosecuted for coercive and controlling behaviour in the year ending December 2017 were male (ONS, 2018).

- Analysis of Merseyside Police domestic abuse data found that 95% of coercive control victims were women and 74% of perpetrators were men. 76% of coercive control cases happened within an intimate partner context. The study found that common abusive behaviours used in coercive control included "…use of technology (such as phone trackers, controlling social media usage, barrage of text messages or monitoring phone usage), sexual coercion, monitoring behaviours, isolation, threats, financial abuse, deprivation (depriving access to support) and physical violence (63% of coercive control cases featured reports of physical violence)". (Barlow et al, 2018).

- One study found that 95 out of 100 domestic abuse survivors reported experiencing coercive control. (Kelly et al, 2014)

- Another study found that women are far more likely than men to be victims of abuse that involves ongoing degradation and frightening threats – two key elements of coercive control (Myhill, 2015).

*February 2019*

**www.womensaid.org.uk**

# Coercive control incidents double in a year, as campaigners warn domestic abuse 'remains at epidemic levels'

By Gabriella Swerling, Social and Religious Affairs Editor

Coercive control reports to police have doubled within a year, new figures reveal, as campaigners warn that the true extent of the crime is only just starting to be recognised.

There were 17,616 offences of coercive control recorded by the police in the year ending March 2019, compared with 9,053 in the year ending March 2018, the Office for National Statistics (ONS) said.

Charities and campaigners have welcomed the increasing awareness surrounding coercive control, but have also warned that domestic abuse "remains at epidemic levels".

It was not until 2015 that coercive control was officially criminalised in law and recognised as a form of domestic abuse.

The term became mainstream after earlier this summer, Sally Challen, who had been in prison for almost a decade, became the first person to successfully use it as a defence after the Crown Prosecution Service (CPS) accepted her plea of manslaughter on the grounds of diminished responsibility.

The 65-year-old mother-of-two bludgeoned her abusive husband to death in a hammer attack in the kitchen of their Surrey home in August 2010 after decades of being coerced and humiliated by him.

Mrs Challen's son, David, who successfully campaigned for his mother's freedom, told *The Telegraph*: "The significant increase in cases of coercive control offences reported is a vital step forward in domestic abuse.

'However, it is even more vital to listen to these victims who've come forward and recognise that this form of abuse is as severe as physical violence. It is up to the police and the criminal courts to start instilling that trust if we're to continue to gain victims' confidence coming forward.'

Coercive control is a form of behaviour designed to make a person dependent by isolating them from support, exploiting them, depriving them of independence and regulating their everyday behaviour. It usually manifests itself in an act or a pattern of acts of assault, threats, humiliation and intimidation or other abuse that is used to harm, punish or frighten their victim.

The ONS said that the increase in the number of coercive control offences "are common for new offences" and the rise could be attributed to "improvements in recognising incidents of coercive control by the police and using the new law accordingly".

Researchers also reported that there were a total of 1,316,800 domestic abuse-related incidents and crimes recorded by the police in England and Wales in the year ending March 2019, up 118,706 from the previous year.

Of these, 746,219 were subsequently recorded as crimes, up from 599,549 in the previous year – a volume increase of 146,670 (24%).

However police only made 98,470 referrals to the Crown Prosecution Service (CPS) for suspects in domestic abuse-related cases to be charged, down from 110,653 the previous year.

There were also 366 domestic homicides recorded by the police in England and Wales between April 2016 and March 2018, accounting for 20% of all killings of victims aged over 16.

Deputy Chief Constable Louisa Rolfe, who leads the National Police Chiefs' Council's work on domestic abuse, said the fall in charging referrals was "concerning" and it was working with the CPS to "understand the complex reasons for this."

She added: "The large increases in reporting comes alongside more complex and demanding investigations and the pressure on police resources.

'Arrests and prosecutions may provide a temporary respite for victims but a public health response is vital to keep people safe and provide a lasting solution.'

Adina Claire, Acting Co-Chief Executive of Women's Aid, added: 'It is encouraging that the coercive control legislation is being used more and that recorded incidents have almost doubled.

'However, domestic abuse remains at epidemic levels, with an estimated 1.6 million women experiencing domestic abuse last year alone. Despite this, police are making fewer referrals to the CPS and there has been a decrease in the proportion of female victims reporting domestic abuse to the police.

'What these statistics show is that, while domestic abuse can happen to anyone, women experience the most severe and repeated forms of abuse. 84% of homicide victims killed by a current or former partner are female, which shows why specialist refuge services for women, including expert services for BME women, have to exist.'

*25 November 2019*

# Domestic abuse in England and Wales overview: November 2019

Latest bulletin from The Office for National Statistics.

## Main points

◆ The latest figures from the Crime Survey for England and Wales show little change in the prevalence of domestic abuse in recent years.

◆ In the year ending March 2019, an estimated 2.4 million adults aged 16 to 74 years experienced domestic abuse in the last year (1.6 million women and 786,000 men).

◆ The police recorded 746,219 domestic abuse-related crimes in the year ending March 2019, an increase of 24% from the previous year.

◆ This increase may reflect improved recording by the police and increased reporting by victims.

◆ The police made 32 arrests per 100 domestic abuse-related crimes in the year ending March 2019, equating to 214,965 arrests (in the 39 police forces that supplied data).

◆ Referrals of suspects of domestic abuse-flagged cases from the police to the Crown Prosecution Service (CPS) for a charging decision fell 11%, from 110,653 in the year ending March 2018 to 98,470 in the year ending March 2019.

◆ The charging rate[1] in the year ending March 2019 was 74%, a small decrease compared with the previous year (76%).

◆ Over three-quarters of domestic abuse-related CPS prosecutions were successful in securing a conviction in the year ending March 2019 (77%), a similar level to the previous year.

◆ Over 60% of referrals made to independent domestic violence advisor services were made by the police in the year ending March 2018.

## Statistician's comment

Commenting on today's domestic abuse figures, an ONS statistician said:

'There has been little change in the prevalence of domestic abuse estimated by the crime survey in the last year. Although the number of crimes recorded by the police has increased by nearly a quarter in the past year, this may reflect improvements in police recording and an increase in victims' willingness to come forward.

'Of those crimes that were recorded by the police, fewer suspects were referred to the Crown Prosecution Service than the previous year. For those that appeared before the court, more than three-quarters resulted in a conviction for the perpetrator of the abuse.'

Notes for: Main points
1. The charging rate is the number of suspects of CPS domestic abuse-flagged cases that were charged as a proportion of all those that resulted in a legal decision.

## Analysis of domestic abuse data

### Latest figures

According to the Crime Survey for England and Wales (CSEW) year ending March 2019, an estimated 5.7% of adults aged 16 to 74 years (2.4 million people) experienced domestic abuse in the last year (Figure 1). A higher percentage of adults experienced abuse carried out by a partner or ex-partner (4.2%) than by a family member (2.0%).

The police recorded a total of 1,316,800 domestic abuse-related incidents and crimes in England and Wales in the year ending March 2019. Of these, 43% (570,581) were incidents not subsequently recorded as a crime. The remaining 57% (746,219) were recorded as domestic abuse-related crimes.

## Trends over time

There was no significant difference in the prevalence of domestic abuse for men and women aged 16 to 59 years[1] in the year ending March 2019 compared with the year ending March 2018. However, primarily driven by a significant decrease in the year ending March 2009, the prevalence is significantly lower than that reported for the year ending March 2005 (Figure 2). For example, 4.2% of men and 8.4% of women aged 16 to 59 years had experienced domestic abuse within the last year in the year ending March 2019. This compared with 6.5% of men and 11.1% of women in the year ending March 2005.

Notes for: Analysis of domestic abuse data

1. The age range for respondents eligible for the domestic abuse, sexual assault and stalking self-completion module of the Crime Survey for England and Wales was expanded in April 2017, changing from adults aged 16 to 59 years to adults aged 16 to 74 years. Where analysis requires more than the last two years of data, the 16 to 59 years age range is used.

*25 November 2019*

## Figure 1: A higher percentage of adults were victims of partner abuse than family abuse

Prevalence of domestic abuse in the last year for adults aged 16 to 74 years, by perpetrator-relationship, England and Wales, year ending March 2019

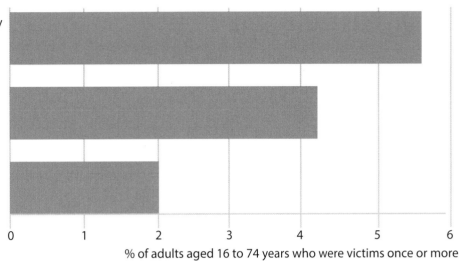

Any domestic abuse (partner or family non-physical abuse; threats; force; sexual assault or stalking)
Any partner abuse (non-physical abuse; threats; force; sexual assault or stalking)
Any family abuse (non-physical abuse; threats; force; sexual assault or stalking)
0
1
2
3
4
5
6
% of adults aged 16 to 74 years who were victims once or more


Source: Office for National Statistics – Crime Survey for England and Wales

## Figure 2: There was no change in the prevalence of domestic abuse in the last year

Prevalence of domestic abuse in the last year for adults aged 16 to 59 years, England and Wales, year ending March 2005 to year ending March 2019

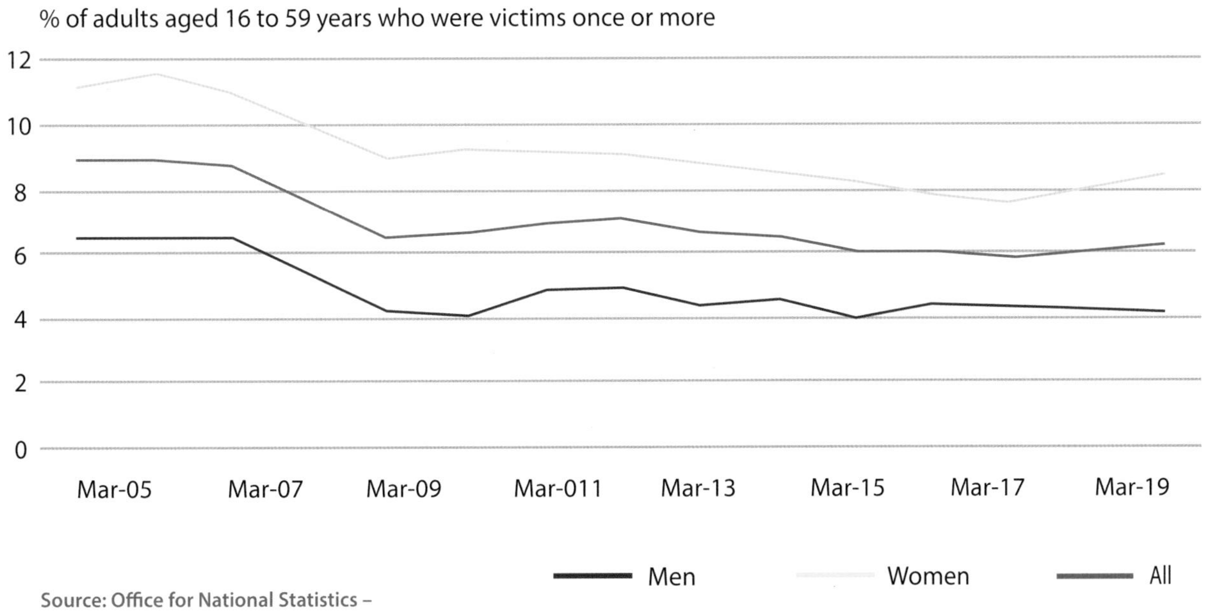

% of adults aged 16 to 59 years who were victims once or more
12
10
8
6
4
2
0
Mar-05
Mar-07
Mar-09
Mar-011
Mar-13
Mar-15
Mar-17
Mar-19
Men
Women
All


Source: Office for National Statistics – Crime Survey for England and Wales



www.ons.gov.uk

# Domestic abuse in Scotland: 2018-2019 statistics

Characteristics of victims and perpetrators of domestic abuse incidents recorded by the police in Scotland.

## Key points

- Levels of domestic abuse recorded by the police in Scotland have remained relatively stable since 2011-12, with around 58,000 to 61,000 incidents a year. The police recorded 60,641 incidents of domestic abuse in 2018-19, an increase of 2% compared to the previous year.

- In 2018-19, 41% of incidents of domestic abuse recorded by the police in Scotland included the recording of at least one crime or offence.

- The type of crime or offence that was most frequently recorded as part of a domestic abuse incident in 2018-19 was Common assault (accounting for 36% of all crimes and offences recorded). This was followed by Breach of the peace etc. accounting for 29% of crimes and offences.

- There were 112 incidents of domestic abuse recorded by the police in Scotland per 10,000 population in 2018-19. At a local authority level, Dundee City (157), West Dunbartonshire (148) and Glasgow City (147) recorded the highest incident rates per 10,000 population. The Shetland Islands (52) and East Renfrewshire (54) recorded the lowest rates per 10,000 population.

- Where gender information was recorded, around four out of every five incidents of domestic abuse in 2018-19 had a female victim and a male accused. This proportion has remained very stable since 2011-12.

- In 2018-19, 16% of domestic abuse incidents involved a male victim and a female accused (where gender was recorded). Again, this proportion has remained stable since 2011-12 (ranging from 16% to 18%).

- In 2018-19, the 26-30 years old age group had the highest incident rate for victims (263 incidents recorded per 10,000 population). The 31-35 years old age group had the highest incident rate for the accused (246 incidents recorded per 10,000 population).

- Recorded incidents of domestic abuse were higher on a Saturday or Sunday than on any other day of the week (with these two days together accounting for 35% of incidents in 2018-19).

- In 2018-19, 88% of all domestic abuse incidents occurred in a home or dwelling.

*25 February 2020*

# Domestic abuse recorded by the police in Scotland, 2018-2019

## WHO were the victims?

In 2018-19, more than **4 out of 5** (83%) victims of domestic abuse were female.

## WHAT was the gender of the victims and accused

**82%** of incidents involved a female victim and a male accused.

**16%** of incidents involved a male victim and a female accused.

In the remaining **2%** of cases, both the victim and accused were the same gender.

## 60,641

Incidents of domestic abuse were recorded by the police in 2018-19.

● rates above the Scottish average

## WHERE did incidents occur

**88%** of domestic abuse incidents occurred in a home or dwelling.

**39%** of domestic abuse incidents occurred in the victim's home.

## WHEN did incidents occur?

Sat
Sun

**35%** of domestic abuse incidents occurred at the weekend.

| M | T | W | T | F | S | S |
|---|---|---|---|---|---|---|
| 13% | 13% | 13% | 13% | 14% | 17% | 18% |

Source: Justice Analytical Services

# Jess Phillips MP: The Domestic Abuse Bill is to be welcomed, but there is still work to be done

The long-awaited Domestic Abuse Bill contains some good measures – but there is still a way to go to ensure proper protection for victims, writes Jess Phillips MP.

The Domestic Abuse Bill is to be welcomed. I have for the past three years felt like a 5-year-old in the back of the car who asks as every mile of a journey passes, "are we nearly there yet?". The assurance that, "we expect the second reading of the bill to be before Easter" has been said to me for two years and I am only kicking myself that I didn't ask ministers which year or even which decade they meant. I really hope that all the false starts, prorogations and, "it just needs a bit more work" days are done, and we will see this bill in front of the House and scrutinised properly and in public at last.

The bill has some good stuff in it, placing domestic abuse secure accommodation and refuge on a statutory footing, and demanding that all tier one local authorities (county councils and unitary authorities) must provide it. It appears to be coming with money to do it too. Big tick. Of course, only a very small percentage of victims and their children ever go into a refuge and the majority of support provided for domestic abuse victims is in the community and relies on the availability of social housing. These are less well catered for in the bill currently and so it will need some work on this.

'The Government is going to have to decide do they want to help victims of violence and abuse more than they want to look tough on migrants'

Another big tick in the bill is that it finally is banning the cross examination by perpetrators of domestic and sexual abuse of their victims in the family court. This ban is only needed because the Conservative government's decimation of legal aid has led to the rise of litigants in person in civil courts across the land. But hey, I have been campaigning for this particular sticking plaster for a long time and it has fallen more times than the Domestic Abuse Bill itself, as it was originally in the Prisons and Courts Bill which fell when Theresa May was trigger happy with elections.

Unfortunately, the bill in its current form does not yet truly transform the experience of victims of abuse in our family courts. We will have to wait until a review of this part of our justice system concludes before we see it reflected in legislation. For me, the bill will fail to protect in the area of family law unless there is a very clear change in legislation regarding the presumption of contact with a violent partner. Anyone who has read the Nineteen Child Homicides report authored by Women's Aid will know that that presumption has cost children their lives and women their children. Ministers have assured us that they will have their review done before report stage of the Bill and, hey they have never been wrong about timelines before! Oh.

The biggest area of contention which has been raised again and again throughout the build up to the bill is how it handles migrant women and children who are victims of domestic abuse, especially those with no recourse to public funds. Pretty much every specialist charity has called for changes to the law for this vulnerable group. The APPG on Domestic Abuse undertook a review which concluded that the bill must address this issue, and the Joint Committee chaired by Maria Miller recommended the same. However, the bill is still failing to address the very real concerns about how migrant victims suffer destitution and barriers to support, which is in some cases killing them. This is undoubtedly the Government's blind spot, and as the bill goes through parliament they are going to have to decide, do they want to help victims of violence and abuse more than they want to look tough on migrants? I hope it is the former. I am near certain it will be the latter.

The Domestic Abuse Bill could be ground-breaking or it could just move the ground a little. The Government's majority means that they will ultimately get to decide which it is – I hope they choose wisely.

*9 March 2020*

Jess Phillips is Labour MP for Birmingham Yardley and associate editor of *The House.* This article appeared in *The House Magazine*, issue 1675

# Challenging the myths

Domestic abuse is a crisis that affects us all, and it has devastating impacts; on average two women every week are killed by a partner or ex-partner in England and Wales. This must change.

*There are many myths around domestic abuse and its causes. Women's Aid is challenging some of the most widely-believed and deep-rooted misconceptions.*

**Myth #1: Alcohol and drugs make men more violent.**

**Reality:** Alcohol and drugs can make existing abuse worse, or be a catalyst for an attack, but they do not cause domestic abuse. Many people use alcohol or drugs and do not abuse their partner, so it should never be used to excuse violent or controlling behaviour. The perpetrator alone is responsible for his actions.

**Myth #2: If it was that bad, she'd leave.**

**Reality:** Women stay in abusive relationships for many different reasons, and it can be very difficult for a woman to leave an abusive partner – even if she wants to. Like any other relationship, one that ends in abuse began with falling in love and being in love. Abuse rarely starts at the beginning of a relationship, but when it is established and often harder to leave.

A woman may still be in love with her partner and believe him when he says he is sorry and it won't happen again; she may be frightened for her life or for the safety of her children if she leaves; she may have nowhere to go; she may have no financial independence. Abusers often isolate their partners from family and friends in order to control them, making it even more difficult for an abused woman to exit the relationship.

Women in abusive relationships need support and understanding – not judgement.

**Myth #3: Domestic abuse always involves physical violence.**

**Reality:** Domestic abuse does not always include physical violence. Women's Aid defines domestic abuse as an incident or pattern of incidents of controlling, coercive, threatening, degrading and violent behaviour, including sexual violence, by a partner or ex-partner. These incidents can include coercive control; psychological and/or emotional abuse; physical abuse; sexual abuse; financial abuse; harassment; stalking; and/or online or digital abuse.

**Myth #4: He can be a good father even if he abuses his partner – the parents' relationship doesn't have to affect the children.**

**Reality:** An estimated 90% of children whose mothers are abused witness the abuse. The effects are traumatic and long-lasting. When a child witnesses domestic abuse, this is child abuse. Between 40% and 70% of these children are also direct victims of the abuse which is happening at home.

### Myth #5: She provoked him.

**Reality:** This myth is widespread and deep-rooted. It is often based on the belief that the man is the head of the family, and that his role is to punish his partner or children if they act in a way he doesn't approve of.

The myth is dangerous because any reference to 'provocation' means that we are blaming the woman and relieving the abuser of responsibility for his actions.

Abuse or violence of any kind is never the victim's fault. Responsibility always lies with the perpetrator, and with him alone.

### Myth #6: Domestic abuse is a private family matter, and not a social issue.

**Reality:** Violence and abuse against women and children incurs high costs for society: hospital treatment, medication, court proceedings, lawyers' fees, imprisonment – not to mention the psychological and physical impact on those who experience it.

All too often, when women disclose their abuse, no one listens to them, and no one asks them what they would like to happen next. That's why Women's Aid have launched a new approach for domestic abuse survivors and their children: *Change that Lasts*. It places the survivor at the heart and builds responses around her needs and the strengths and resources available to her.

Domestic abuse happens every single day all over the world, and affects women of all ages, classes and backgrounds. It is a serious, widespread crime. Despite this, Women's Aid and other organisations like us are still campaigning to ensure that survivors' voices are heard. When we describe domestic abuse as a 'private family matter', we minimise, condone and permit it.

### Myth #7: Pornography is not linked to violence against women.

**Reality:** Most consumers of pornography are male, and pornographic material is becoming increasingly explicit, violent and focused on male pleasure. It's also freely available to anyone online, and studies indicate it is how many young people find out about sex.

Pornography contributes to a culture of misogyny, in which women and girls are abused by men for male pleasure. Women are harmed by pornography in two ways: directly, when they are used for the production of pornographic material; and indirectly, through the effects of mainstream availability and consumption of violent pornography.

### Myth #8: Women are just as abusive as men.

**Reality:** In the vast majority of cases, domestic abuse is experienced by women and perpetrated by men. Two women a week are murdered by a current or ex-partner in England and Wales alone. Of the 92,779 domestic abuse court prosecutions last year, 92.4% of defendants were male, and 84% of victims were female. It is a gendered crime which is deeply rooted in the societal inequality between women and men.

Women are more likely than men to experience multiple incidents of abuse, different types of domestic abuse, and sexual violence particularly.

Domestic abuse exists as part of the wider spectrum of violence against women and girls, which also includes different forms of family violence such as forced marriage, female genital mutilation and so-called "honour crimes" that are perpetrated primarily by family members.

## Myth #9: Women often lie about abuse.

**Reality:** False allegations about domestic abuse are extremely rare. The Crown Prosecution Service released the first ever study of this in 2013, and concluded that false allegations are even more infrequent than previously thought. In the 17 month period that the study examined, there were 111,891 prosecutions for domestic violence, and only six prosecutions for making false allegations.

This myth is extremely damaging, because the fear of being called a liar can and does deter women from reporting the abuse they have experienced.

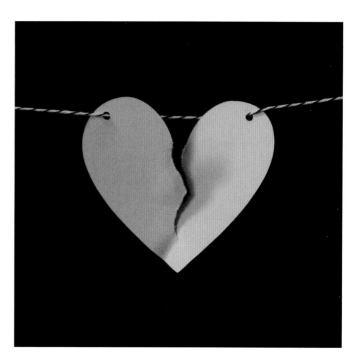

## Myth #10: Men who abuse women are mentally unwell.

**Reality:** There is no research that supports this myth. Abuse and violence are a choice, and there is no excuse for them. Domestic abuse happens throughout every level of society, regardless of health, wealth or status.

## Myth #11: Women are attracted to abusive men.

Reality: Domestic abuse is prevalent throughout society, and it is not uncommon for a woman to experience abuse in more than one relationship. To suggest that some women are particularly attracted to abusive men is victim-blaming. A perpetrator of domestic abuse can be charming and charismatic when he first meets a new partner, and often no one, let alone the woman he has just met, would suspect he would ever be abusive in a relationship.

## Myth #12: Men who abuse their partners saw their fathers abuse their mothers.

**Reality:** Domestic abuse is prevalent throughout society, and because of this many people have grown up witnessing domestic abuse. Most of these people will never perpetrate domestic abuse in their own relationships, so it is never an excuse – and some of our most passionate supporters are child survivors of domestic abuse.

## Myth #13: Domestic abuse isn't that common.

**Reality:** We know through our work over the last 42 years with survivors and local services that domestic abuse is very common. On average a woman is killed by her male partner or former partner every four days in the UK England and Wales. Domestic abuse has a higher rate of repeat victimisation than any other crime, and on average, the police receive over 100 emergency calls relating to domestic abuse every hour.

The *2014/15 Crime Survey of England and Wales* found that, overall, 27.1% of women (an estimated 4.5 million women) have experienced domestic abuse since the age of sixteen.

## Myth #14: Domestic abuse is a 'crime of passion', a momentary loss of control.

**Reality:** Domestic abuse is rarely about losing control, but taking control. Abusive men rarely act spontaneously when angry. They consciously choose when to abuse their partner: when they are alone, and when there are no witnesses (if there is a witness, then usually they are a child). He has control over whom he abuses.

## Myth #15: All couples argue – it's not domestic abuse, it's just a normal relationship.

**Reality:** Abuse and disagreement are not the same things. Different opinions are normal and completely acceptable in healthy relationships. Abuse is not a disagreement – it is the use of physical, sexual, emotional or psychological violence or threats in order to govern and control another person's thinking, opinions, emotions and behaviour.

When abuse is involved, there is no discussion between equals. There is fear of saying or doing the 'wrong' thing.

## Myth #16: Women are more likely to be attacked by strangers than by those who claim to love them.

**Reality:** In fact, the opposite is true. Women are far more likely to be assaulted, raped and murdered by men known to them than by strangers.

According to Rape Crisis, only around 10% of rapes are committed by men unknown to the victim. Women are far likelier to be attacked by a man they know and trust.

*February 2019*

# Statistics: Violence in Scotland

In 2017-2018 there were 59,541 incidents of domestic abuse recorded by Police Scotland. Women made up 82% of the victims[1].

In 2018-19 there were:

◆ 2,426 cases of rape and attempted rape reported to Police Scotland.[1]

◆ 5,123 cases of sexual assault reported to Police Scotland.[1]

◆ 8% increase in sexual crimes from 12,487 to 13,547. The recording of these crimes is at the highest level seen since 1971, the first year for which comparable groups are available.[1]

◆ While figures for many crimes in Scotland are going down, for sexual offences they continue to rise. Sexual crimes have been on a long-term upward trend since 1974, and have increased each consecutive year since 2008-09. Sexual crimes are at the highest level seen since 1971, the first year for which comparable crime groups are available.[1]

The actual figures are higher than these statistics suggest due to low reporting of these crimes. Scottish Crime and Justice Survey 2014 – 2015 showed that only 16.8% of people who were victim-survivors of rape reported it to the police.[2]

One in ten women in Scotland has experienced rape & one in five women in Scotland has had someone try to make them have sex against their will.[3]

Research indicates that only 58% of people in Scotland believe that a woman who wears revealing clothing on a night out is 'not at all to blame' for being raped, with 60% saying the same of a woman who is very drunk. Around a quarter think that 'women often lie about being raped' and nearly 2 in 5 believe that 'rape results from men being unable to control their need for sex'.[4]

35% of women do not feel safe walking alone in their neighbourhood after dark.[5]

## Exacerbated by other forms of inequality

Disabled women are twice as likely to experience men's violence as non-disabled women.[6]

83% of trans women have experienced hate crime at some point in their lives.[7]

Black and minority ethnic (BME) and migrant women face higher levels of domestic homicide and abuse driven suicide.[8]

## Low conviction rates

In 2016-17, the conviction rate for rape and attempted rape fell to the lowest level since 2008/09. In a year where there were 1,878 rapes and attempted rapes reported to the police, there were only 98 convictions.

In 2016-17, there were 58,810 domestic abuse incidents reported to the police – an increase of 1% from the previous year. 30,630 were dealt with by prosecutors, there were 10,830 convictions, a 12% decrease from 2015-16, the lowest level since 2012/2013.

## Violence worldwide

Globally, as many as 38% of murders of women are committed by a male intimate partner.[9]

A wide scale European study carried out by the EU Agency for Fundamental Rights in 2014 found that an estimated 83 million to 102 million women (45 per cent to 55 per cent of women) in the EU-28 have experienced sexual harassment since the age of 15.[10]

## Cost of VAWG (Violence Against Women and Girls)

Scottish Government estimates, based on a study in England, found that domestic abuse costs the Scottish public purse £2.3 billion while VAWG costs Scotland £4 billion.

VAWG costs England's NHS an estimated £2.9 billion every year. The cost per person of providing cognitive trauma therapy was estimated at £1,600.

Mental health VAWG, including emotional abuse and coercive control, has been linked to a greater risk of adverse mental health outcomes among women. The most prevalent include depression, suicide attempts, post-traumatic stress, other stress and anxiety conditions, sleeping or eating disorders and psychosomatic conditions. Many of the physical health impacts of VAWG will also have direct implications for women's mental health.

## Gender inequality

51% of the population of Scotland are women. Yet women make up only:

- 35% of MSPs, 25% of local councillors, 16% of council leaders, 17% of MEPs.

- 28% of public body chief executives, 26% of university principals, 23% of sheriffs,

- 7% of senior police officers.

- 0% of major newspaper editors, 19% of major museums and art galleries directors, 14% of national sports bodies chief executives, 0% of CEOs of 'top' businesses.[11]

On average women in Scotland earn £182.90 per week less than men.[12]

Women are four times more likely than men to give up paid work to do unpaid care work.[13]

The economic value of the unpaid care provided by women in the UK is estimated to be £77bn per year.[14]

Violence against women is caused by gender inequality, and it allows this inequality to continue.

1 Recorded Crime in Scotland 2017-2018 bulletin (www.gov.scot)

2 Recorded crime in Scotland : 2018 -2019

3 Scottish Crime & Justice Survey 2014/15: Sexual Victimisation & Stalking

4 www.rapecrisisscotland.org.uk

5 Scottish Social Attitudes Survey 2014: Attitudes to violence against women in Scotland

6 Daisie Project Violence Against Disabled Women Survey (www.womenssupportproject.co.uk)

7 Scottish LGBTI hate crime report 2017

8 Southall Black Sisters - Safe and Sane Report 2011

9 WHO Violence Against Women publication 2017

10 Violence against women: an EU-wide survey. Results at a glance 2014

11 Engender Sex & Power in Scotland 2017 publication

12 Close the Gap www.closethegap.org.uk

13 www.fawcettsociety.org.uk

14 Carers UK www.carersuk.org

# 'A national travesty': Domestic abuse rises 24% as number of cases passed for charge falls 11%

'Domestic abuse is such a devastating crime, the women who experience it lose everything: their home, their freedom, their dignity and ultimately their lives.'

By Maya Oppenheim, Women's Correspondent

Domestic abuse has risen by 24 per cent in a year while referrals of cases from the police to the Crown Prosecution Service fell by 11 per cent.

New figures show police recorded an average of one incident of domestic abuse per minute in the year ending March 2019.

Some 746,219 domestic abuse-related crimes were recorded in total – a rise of almost a quarter on the previous year.

A charity working with victims of domestic abuse described the rising trends as a 'national travesty'.

The data, released by the Office for National Statistics (ONS), showed referrals of suspects from domestic abuse-flagged cases to the CPS for a charging decision fell 11 per cent from 110,653 to 98,470 from the previous year.

An estimated 1.6 million women aged 16 to 74 years experienced domestic abuse in the year ending March 2019, according to the new figures.

The number of recorded coercive control offences were found to have nearly doubled within the past year.

The law changed in 2015 to recognise psychological manipulation, or coercive control, as a form of domestic abuse. Some 9,053 offences were recorded in the year ending March 2018, but had climbed to 17,616 by March this year.

Sarika Seshadri, of lead domestic abuse charity Women's Aid, said: 'The data shows domestic abuse is persistently high. The fall in cases being referred to the CPS is very troubling – especially when we know how difficult it is to come forward. Women need to know when they come forward that these cases are dealt with effectively.

'Domestic abuse is such a devastating crime, the women who experience it lose everything: their home, their freedom, their dignity and ultimately their lives. We do have a word of caution because the stats do not capture the gendered nature of domestic abuse. The gender breakdown doesn't capture the context in which incidents took place or the impact it had on someone. It also doesn't show whether incidents happen more than once or their severity.

'The breakdown doesn't adequately capture the fact that women disproportionately experience domestic violence or the fact women experience higher rates of repeated victimisation and are far more likely to be seriously hurt or killed than men who experience domestic abuse.'

Ms Seshadri argued the new data does not capture the scale of the problem, because victims do not always come forward.

The head of research at the charity said domestic abuse was a 'critical issue' for wider society – saying it causes 'suffering, fear and long-term damage' to relationships, families and communities, as well as costing the economy a 'staggering' £66bn a year.

Adina Claire, acting co-chief executive of Women's Aid, said it had reached 'epidemic levels'.

The latest figures, which use data from the Crime Survey for England and Wales, found 84 per cent of all victims killed by a partner or former partner are female. The suspect was male in all but two cases.

Sandra Horley, of Refuge, the largest provider of specialist domestic violence services in the UK, said: "These statistics should serve as a serious wake-up call to the future government that domestic abuse is a major crime in this country and must be top of the political agenda.

'It is clear that the likelihood of women and girls experiencing domestic abuse at some point in their lives is increasing. This is devastating news given this time last year we knew one in four women would experience domestic abuse – this figure is edging towards one in three. Alarmingly, incidents of domestic sexual assault are also increasing. This rise is set against a backdrop of lower conviction rates. These statistics are a national travesty.'

The latest figures show the police made 32 arrests for every 100 domestic abuse-related crimes in the year ending March 2019 – amounting to 214,965 arrests in total.

A spokesperson for the ONS said: 'Although the number of crimes recorded by the police has increased by nearly a

quarter in the past year, this may reflect improvements in police recording and an increase in victims' willingness to come forward.'

Deputy Chief Constable Louisa Rolfe, the National Police Chiefs' Council lead for domestic abuse, said police have worked hard to improve their response to domestic abuse over recent years and this is indicated in statistics that reveal increased reporting and better recording.

She said: 'In the past, many verbal arguments were recorded as an incident and not a crime, yet technically these can be a common assault, a harassment or threat of violence. These may have little prospect of a prosecution but recording them allows dedicated domestic abuse officers to safeguard victims, build evidence and recognise patterns.

'Part of the increase is also down to better identification and reporting of domestic abuse, particularly coercive and controlling behaviour. We are continuing to improve our response to this to bring more offenders to justice.

'The fall in the proportion of domestic abuse crimes being referred for a charging decision is concerning and we are working with the CPS to understand the complex reasons for this. The large increases in reporting come alongside more complex and demanding investigations and the pressure on police resources.'

Ms Rolfe argued the way police react to domestic abuse only forms one element of the answer – adding that arrests and prosecutions may deliver a 'temporary respite' for survivors, but a public health response is imperative to ensure people remain safe and a long-term solution is delivered.

*25 November 2019*

# Over half of UK women killed by men die at hands of partner or ex

Femicide Census for 2018 shows 149 women killed, the highest number since census began.

By Laith Al-Khalaf and Alexandra Topping

**M**ore than half the women killed by men in the UK in 2018 were killed by a current or former partner, many after they had taken steps to leave, according to a report on femicide.

The fourth Femicide Census, conducted by the campaigner Karen Ingala Smith, found 149 women were killed by 147 men in 2018. The number of deaths is an increase of 10 on the previous year and the highest number since the census began.

Of the deceased women, 91 (61%) were killed by a current or former partner. Only 6% of murders were committed by a stranger.

Of the 58 women not killed by current or former partners, 12 were killed by their sons or stepsons, while five were killed by a son-in-law or former son-in-law.

In half the cases, perpetrators had previous histories of violence against the victim or other women, with three men found to have killed before. One had been convicted of manslaughter in 1996 and jailed for three years. The second, who also had a history of stalking, had been released from prison in 2014 after murdering his previous partner in 1999. The third had been convicted of culpable homicide in 1992 and had also been convicted of serious violent offences in 2001 and 2010.

The most common method of murder was a sharp instrument, with strangulation or asphyxiation the second most common. The majority of killings (68%) occurred either in or immediately around the woman's house.

Ingala Smith, who runs the domestic violence charity Nia, said many of the women had expressed fear and warnings about their killer to police, other services and friends and family.

Of the women killed in 2018, 41% of those killed by a current or former partner had left or were in the process of leaving – with 30% of these women killed within the first month and 70% killed within the first year after separation.

'It's important that we challenge received wisdom about seeing leaving a violent relationship being a straightforward way that women can remove themselves from the danger of a violent partner,' Ingala Smith said.

The report, released on Thursday, found that "overkilling" – defined as the use of excessive, gratuitous violence beyond that necessary to cause the victim's death – was evident in 56% of cases.

Younger women aged between 26 and 35 were more likely to be subjected to extreme, gratuitous violence, according to the report. It added that while such attacks were often described as "frenzied" and resulting from a "loss of control", the evidence suggested that was not the case.

'In one femicide, the postmortem carried out on the victim established that most of the 70-plus stab wounds inflicted were very shallow, indicating a high degree of control and suggesting the perpetrator's intent to torture the victim before inflicting the fatal wounds,' the report said.

The Femicide Census produces a report every year of women killed by men in the UK. It aims to provide "data on the killings of women by men and aims to highlight patterns and trends which can feed into policy and service responses and in particular prevention and early intervention", according to the report.

'There is a high degree of normalisation of men's violence against women and no end of excuses or rationales assumed and extended to perpetrators often without foundation,' said Ingala Smith, a co-founder of the census.

She added that closure and under-resourcing of specialist women-only services meant there was little option for some women looking to leave "violent, controlling and abusive relationships".

*20 February 2020*

# Attacks on family members by women rise twice as fast as by men, new report shows

By Verity Bowman

**A**ttacks by women on family members have risen twice as fast as those by men, new data show, leading campaigners to call for an overhaul of approaches to domestic violence.

Female perpetrators now account for 28 per cent of cases - compared to 19 per cent a decade ago. Male perpetrators were still identified in the majority of domestic violence incidents.

The number of attacks committed by females has tripled, growing from 27,762 in 2009 to 92,409 in 2018, according to the data obtained by The Sunday Telegraph under the Freedom of Information Act. More than 10,000 incidents were identified by police in West Yorkshire alone.

It is thought a significant number of domestic violence incidents still go unreported.

Experts last night called for an overhaul of approaches to abuse, arguing domestic violence cannot be thought of as a male only crime.

Mark Brooks, chairman of the Mankind Initiative, which supports male victims of domestic abuse, said: "These figures are a wake-up call on why, when we think of domestic abuse, although the gender and age of victims is important it should be no more significant than them as an individual.

'These figures uncover the extent of abuse committed by women and confirm what many of us in the domestic abuse sector already know about the level of domestic abuse carried out by women.'

Mr Brooks added that current approaches to domestic abuse are defined by the belief it 'is a gendered crime', resulting in a 'female victims first' approach that often leaves those suffering abuse at the hands of women behind.

He believes the increase in female perpetrators is because the 'stigma of being victim of a female' has decreased, but the sector needs to 'modernise' too by becoming more inclusive of male and LGBTQ+ victims.

'We've progressed to the 21st century in many areas, but in terms of approaches to domestic abuse, we still struggle to see women as violent.'

On Wednesday, Hull Crown Court heard how one woman stabbed her husband of 40 years with a potato peeler after an argument over a set of blinds. Carol Robinson, 57, pleaded guilty to causing grievous bodily harm after puncturing her husband's lung.

In December, another woman was jailed for four years after stabbing her ex-husband, shouting 'die you b------'.

Joanne Reddy's ex-husband told Manchester Crown Court: 'My physical scars will eventually heal but mental scars never will.'

A 14-year-sentence was given to 44-year-old Nicola Lee in November after she stabbed her partner through the heart in a drunken row. The killer was described as 'manipulating, calculating, dangerous and vicious' after being found guilty of manslaughter. Lee had abused numerous other partners, Newcastle Crown Court heard.

Paul Chivers, 50, was hospitalised by his ex wife after she hit him repeatedly with a hairdryer.

She was convicted of committing grievous bodily harm in 2015 and handed a 18-month prison sentence but, according to Mr Chivers, a 'number of people' found it difficult to view his wife as a violent offender.

'Anybody can be a victim, and anybody can be a perpetrator,' he said. 'It's not a gendered thing anymore, which is the thing people have an issue with.

'I used to go to a church in my town, but the majority of the people in that church took the side of my ex wife. They just didn't understand. They couldn't see how that sort of thing could happen.'

Mr Chivers raised the recent arrest of Caroline Flack to articulate how little perceptions have changed. The Love Island presenter was arrested in December following a domestic incident with her boyfriend, Lewis Burton. 40-year-old Flack has since been charged with assault. She denies the charge.

*25 January 2020*

# Coronavirus lockdown is a dangerous time for victims of domestic abuse – here's what you need to know

**THE CONVERSATION**

An article from The Conversation.

By Nicole Westmarland, Professor of Criminology, Durham University, and Rosnna Bellini, PhD in Digital Civics, Newcastle University

Emphasis is currently being placed on people to self-isolate from their places of work and leisure, posing the home as a place of relative safety during the coronavirus pandemic. However, there is growing concern about what impact this might have on those trapped in intimate relationships with people who use violence and abuse.

For some people, home is not a safe place to be, so the prospect of large parts of the population being confined to prevent the spread of the coronavirus opens the potential for increased incidents of domestic violence.

Of course, COVID-19 cannot cause domestic violence, just as alcohol, drugs, unemployment etc. do not cause it. However, a heightened state of anxiety and stress – including medical anxiety and the stress many of us will feel around being in such close proximity for such extended periods of time with our families – is likely to make this a more dangerous time for women and children. This is in line with existing research that highlights that natural disasters and diseases are factors in increased reports of domestic violence.

Perpetrators may attempt to deal with extra stress and anxiety by imposing stricter and more unrealistic regimes on their families' activities and behaviours. It's a moment when the net of coercive control can be tightened. In fact, 'social distancing' and 'isolation' are core tactics of a coercively controlling partner.

The majority of us are in contact with domestic violence victims, survivors and perpetrators, even if we do not usually recognise it. We are their lecturers, their medical professionals, their carers, their teachers, their social workers, their line managers and so on. If we are working in any kind of support role or direct contact role during the COVID-19 crisis it is important to remember that 'working from home' brings with it very different challenges for different people. We need to be aware of how this may impact victims and perpetrators of domestic violence as well as children in the home.

Here are a few things that we thought might be useful for people to consider during the COVID-19 pandemic:

♦ Understand that stress and anxiety does not cause domestic abuse but it may increase it in families where it is already being perpetrated. Acknowledge that this is an extremely unsafe time.

♦ Check in with someone who you are personally worried about. If making a phone call to a suspected domestic violence victim or survivor, always assume that the perpetrator could be listening in. The same goes for instant messaging services.

♦ If you suspect that the victim or survivor isn't able to talk because of being overheard, give them a readily thought out line to end the call, eg if it is not safe to speak right now then please repeat after me "I'm sorry there is no one called Tina here, you must have got the wrong number."

♦ If it is safe to talk when you call, arrange a codeword or phrase that the victim can use if interrupted, eg if you need to end the call at any point please say 'no, sorry I'm not interested in taking part in the survey'.

## Taking a time out

Where there is not a complete lockdown and people are still able to leave their houses to go for a walk if not ill or in quarantine, the "time out" technique can be used as a last resort to stop immediate physical abuse. If there is a complete lockdown then a garage or garden shed could also work. The time out technique is taught within behaviour change programmes (perpetrator programmes) and is a way of creating physical space during times of escalation. It involves arranging an amount of time (between 45 and 60 minutes) for someone being abusive to physically remove themselves from an environment. They go to a pre-agreed location and message the victim when they are returning to the physical environment. We must underline that this is a last resort to using abuse and should not be treated as a 'cure' for violence.

*19 March 2020*

# Nearly 700 children identified as being at risk of domestic violence every day, figures show

## Councils admit they have no specialist support services in place.

By May Bulman Social Affairs Correspondent

Nearly 700 children are identified as being at risk of domestic violence every day, according to new research which has prompted urgent concerns about the quality of support for these young people.

An analysis of data by Action for Children shows there are on average 692 assessments carried out by children's social services every day where a child is at risk of domestic violence, of which an estimated 611 are being identified as being at risk for the first time.

Separate research into domestic abuse services across England and Wales by the University of Stirling, commissioned by the charity, has meanwhile raised fresh concerns about the level of support on offer specifically for children who have experienced domestic abuse.

The findings show more than one in 10 councils have no specialist support services for children affected, while two thirds say their services for children are at risk in the long-term due to limited funding.

They have prompted campaigners to appeal to politicians for more funding to go to local authorities to support these children and to bring forward legislation that recognises the effect domestic abuse has on families.

It comes as the fate of the Domestic Abuse Bill, which has fallen twice as it passed through parliament to become law – firstly due to the government's prorogation attempt and now because of the General Election – hangs in the balance.

The analysis of figures by Action for Children shows there were 252,580 assessments completed by children's social care services in 2018/19 which identified domestic violence as a factor contributing to the child being in need – meaning on average 692 of these assessments are carried out every day.

Government data from last year data shows there was an average of 1.13 referrals to children's social care per child, indicating that around 611 of these children were being assessed for the first time.

In addition there are many cases of domestic abuse that go unreported, with research by the Children's Commissioner showing 831,000 children in England live in households that report the issue.

It comes amid a dramatic decrease in spending on children and young people's services, with the figure having been axed by nearly £1bn in real terms over the past six years, according to an analysis in 2018.

Meanwhile there has been a 108 per cent surge in child protection enquiries to local authorities, around half of which relate to domestic violence.

Action for Children's chief executive, Julie Bentley, said politicians must not allow children living in the 'terrifying shadow of domestic abuse' to become part of the 'collateral damage' of Brexit.

'Every day our frontline workers see the emotional scars of domestic abuse on children. From nightmares, flashbacks and bed-wetting to depression, or even wanting to end their lives, the effects can last a lifetime,' she said.

'Too many are facing these horrors unnoticed or without the right help, and we have to recognise these children for what they are – victims, not just witnesses.'

The Local Government Association (LGA), which represents councils in England and Wales, said surging demand on children's services meant local authorities were increasingly being forced to prioritise spending for those at immediate risk of harm, rather than on vital earlier support services and prevention schemes.

Katrina Wood, vice chair of the Safer and Stronger Communities Board, added: 'Tackling domestic abuse is an issue that councils take very seriously which is why we support further measures to improve work with local partners to help support more victims and stop this horrendous crime.

'The next government needs to ensure councils have long-term and sustainable funding to help protect children and families from harm.'

Anna Edmundson, NSPCC policy manager, said the current law around the issue was failing to recognise that domestic abuse can 'derail a childhood' and warned of a lack of help for young people who need support.

She added: 'Living with domestic abuse strips away a child's sense of security and can have a devastating impact on their emotional wellbeing and mental health.

'The next government must bring forward legislation that recognises the effect it has on families. Not only that, it must place a duty on local authorities and their partners to make sure specialist services are available to children who have experienced this nightmare.'

*21 November 2019*

# Over 200,000 elderly people experienced domestic abuse in 2017/18

By Abbas Panjwani

On Wednesday, Age UK released findings that at least 200,000 people aged 60 to 74 experienced domestic abuse in England and Wales in 2017/18.

In its coverage of the story, the Daily Mail's print headline claimed that 200,000 elderly people were abused 'by partners'.

This is not what Age UK's report says. Age UK looked at data from the Office for National Statistics' Crime Survey for England and Wales. The Crime Survey defines domestic abuse as abuse by a partner OR by a family member.

The Crime Survey estimates that in 2017/18 152,000 people aged 60 to 74 were victims of partner abuse and 66,000 were victims of family abuse.

The main body of the Daily Mail's article went on to report this correctly.

In all likelihood the number of people experiencing domestic abuse is higher than this, as the Crime Survey does not yet capture the offence of 'coercive and controlling behaviour.'

As we've said before, the scale of domestic abuse is hard to measure accurately. The statistics are compiled through individuals answering questions in a 'self-completion' survey. The figures don't tell us anything about how many individual cases of abuse were experienced by the people responding to the survey. We also don't how many people who have suffered domestic abuse are reluctant or unable to report it in such a survey.

Age UK has called for the definition of domestic abuse to be expanded to include abuse by carers.

*4 October 2019*

# Shedding light on the dark side of teen dating: dating violence

The U.S. is raising awareness about teen dating violence, which is prevalent among teens, often hidden from parents and a risk factor for future problems.

By Dylan Klempner

In the summer of 2002, a month after graduating from high school, Donecia Middleton was physically assaulted by an ex-boyfriend after she called off their relationship. 'He almost killed me,' she said.

Middleton suffered blunt-force trauma to her head and had to be flown to the Brackenridge Trauma Center in Austin, Texas, where she lives. She spent five days in a coma.

She still can't remember what happened. When she woke up in the hospital, she thought she had been in a car accident. Her only information about the assault came from witness statements police later read to her.

Middleton started dating her ex-boyfriend when she was 17. He won her over by saying he would treat her better than her other partners had. Soon, however, he wanted to occupy all of her free time and began separating her from her friends and family.

Looking back, Middleton said she sees a pattern of abuse that started early in the relationship, but 'I never thought he would hit me.' Middleton now works as a domestic-abuse advocate with Love is Respect, providing information and support for young people in dating relationships.

'I hear survivors and victims saying that all the time, like "I never thought that he would hurt me."'

During February, which is Teen Dating Awareness Month, there has been a push in the United States to raise awareness about teen dating violence. U.S. Department of Justice officials, educators and activists are prompting conversations about this often-hidden form of abuse among teenagers.

> 'Teens often tell no one about dating violence.'

According to a national survey of U.S. adults, more than one in three women and one in three men report experiencing sexual violence, physical violence and/or stalking by an intimate partner in their lifetimes. About one in four of the female victims of intimate partner violence and one in seven of the male victims report first experiencing one or more of these forms of violence before the age of 18.

Often, teens who experience dating violence tell no one about the abuse.

Among U.S. high school students, fewer than one in 10 students who reported dating reported experiencing physical violence from a partner in the past year. Meanwhile, eight in 10 parents believe teen-dating violence is not an issue or admit they don't know if it's an issue.

But recent studies show that many teens are being abused online by people they are dating.

Research also shows that victims of dating abuse as adolescents are at higher risk for substance abuse, eating disorders, risky sexual behavior and further domestic violence.

### 'Most parents are unaware.'

On February 15, the U.S. Congress allowed the Violence Against Women Act to lapse because of disagreements between Democrats and Republicans over contentious provisions.

The law provides funding and grants to support victims of domestic violence, dating violence, sexual assault and stalking.

Last summer, Democratic Rep. Sheila Jackson Lee of Texas proposed legislation that would expand the act to include cyber abuse, broaden education and prevention programs and establish protections for Native American women and transgender people. It would also prohibit persons convicted of dating violence from possessing firearms.

### 'The bill would expand the Violence Against Women Act.'

While Congress debates a bipartisan funding bill, 'all legal protections for victims and survivors continue,' the National Task Force to End Domestic Sexual & Domestic Violence wrote in a February 14 statement. Only the act's grant program authorizations expired; the law does not.

The Hill newspaper reported on February 16 that, according to a Democratic aide, 'a full reauthorization is expected to be introduced in March.'

On February 12, Katharine Sullivan, acting director of the Office on Violence Against Women in the U.S. Department of Justice, wrote a blog post honoring Teen Dating Violence Awareness Month and 'emphasizing the seriousness and prevalence of this crime among adolescents.'

Sullivan called attention to her office's youth-focused grant program, the Consolidated Youth Program, which 'provides victim services to teens and works to prevent violence before it ever starts.'

### 'A majority of victims are between 18 and 24.'

She also announced funding for Break the Cycle's Technology Education and Resources Project for Criminal Justice Professionals, which 'trains criminal justice professionals to assist youth victims experiencing abuse or stalking online or via technology.'

Break the Cycle supports young people aged 12 to 24. 'This is an epidemic we've turned away from,' said the organization's CEO, Amy Sanchez, pointing to studies showing that while rates of domestic violence have gone down over the past 20 years, young women remain the most common victims.

'We need to bring this conversation front and center because the vast majority of victims are between the ages of 18 and 24,' Sanchez said.

Break the Cycle provides support to victims such as legal services but also focuses on education and prevention, said Sanchez, whose staff members are mostly in their 20s. 'Young people really have the solutions to ending violence in their own relationships and in society at large.'

Brenna C., who asked that her full name not be used, is also an advocate for Love is Respect. She said she met her ex-boyfriend on the dating website OKCupid when she was 18. It was love at first sight and 'moved super-fast, like abusive relationships a lot of the times do.'

Brenna said her boyfriend dropped out of college and became financially dependent on her, sometimes refusing to pay her back when she took care of shared expenses. 'He would say, "You make more money, so you should pay for more."'

He became verbally abusive, monitored her text messages and social media accounts, woke her up in the middle of the night to argue and threw beer bottles at her. He blamed his behavior on drugs and alcohol.

### 'Threats of suicide are a form of psychological abuse.'

After an argument that became physically abusive, Brenna broke up with him. A couple of months later, he attempted suicide. 'That was really manipulative,' she said.

Threats of suicide in which victims are asked to carry the burden of someone's life and well-being on their shoulders is a form of psychological abuse, said Raychelle Cassada Lohmann, a counselor, educator and author of *The Sexual Trauma Workbook for Teen Girls*. So are isolation and monopolizing all of their partner's time, she said.

'Listen to your friends,' Lohmann advises young people who are starting new relationships. 'They're going to see these things that you may not see.'

## 'Your friends will see things you may not see.'

Lohmann, who practices in North Carolina, said she wants to see more of a focus on prevention, including education programs for youth and their parents.

'Only 55 percent of parents in the United States said that they've had conversations about teen dating violence with their kid. That's low to me,' said Lohmann. 'These should be common conversations that we're having.'

Katie Ray-Jones, CEO of the National Domestic Violence Hotline and Love is Respect, said they provide resources and tools to help parents feel confident about having conversations about healthy relationships, in addition to providing young people with support via phone, live chat and text.

Research shows parents are often the last to hear when their child is in an abusive relationship. 'Our kids aren't necessarily talking to us about themselves,' said Ray-Jones.

She encourages parents to be attuned to changes in their children's behavior, attitudes, dress, social interactions and levels of isolation. 'Those are things parents typically see first.'

## 'You deserve to be kind to yourself.'

Both Sanchez and Ray-Jones said teachers and coaches also use resources from their organizations. Ray-Jones said

teachers have asked their students to pull out their phones in class and connect with Love is Respect online.

School counsellor Lohmann advises teachers to bring up conversations about teen dating abuse more than once a year by weaving it into course curricula. 'When they're reading certain novels that pertain to dating violence or domestic violence, it's a perfect opportunity for teachers to carry that across the curriculum. And it doesn't just have to happen in February.'

Brenna said she wishes there had been more information about dating abuse in school so that she could have spotted red flags. 'I didn't have any kind of education about it when I was growing up,' she said.

'You deserve to be kind to yourself,' Brenna tells young people. 'In a healthy relationship your partner would never want you to change. They just accept you and love you for who you are.'

### THREE QUESTIONS TO CONSIDER:
1. How many Americans report having experienced sexual violence, physical violence or stalking?
2. What are some common signs of dating abuse?
3. What can teachers, parents, friends and policymakers do to prevent teen dating violence?

*21 February 2019*

# Teenagers need to know where love stops and abusive relationships start

Many young women have been in an abusive relationship without even realising. A new website aims to teach them about coercive control.

By Holly Bourne

Why are we always pointing to Instagram as the cause of mental illness in our teenagers? It's frustrating that abusive relationships, and the trauma they cause, are rarely mentioned in discussions about the prevalence of mental health problems in young people. Research by Women's Aid and Cosmopolitan has found that a third of teenage girls have been in an abusive relationship. And, if that isn't shocking enough, when the remaining two-thirds were asked further questions, it emerged that 64% of them had, in fact, experienced abusive behaviour – they just didn't realise it was abuse.

Domestic abuse is normally associated with women cowering on the floor, as a violent husband waits to strike, or mothers covering up their black eyes with concealer before the school run. On the same day that the domestic abuse bill received its second reading in parliament, Age UK called for action to tackle domestic abuse of over-60s, whose needs it says are often overlooked by the law, policy and practice. The needs of teenagers in the heady throes of first love who are in emotionally abusive relationships also need to be recognised.

Common themes of such relationships include (though are not limited to) excessive jealousy, repeated criticism and sexual coercion. If your boyfriend or girlfriend is checking your phone, constantly asking to know your whereabouts, getting upset when you spend time away, turning up unannounced to surprise you, these are all examples of coercive control. If they never apologise in an argument and make everything your fault, tell you what you can and can't wear, undermine you and/or publicly humiliate you under the guise of a "joke", these again are common instances of controlling behaviour. Ditto, if they have a Jekyll/Hyde personality, make you feel like you are walking on eggshells even when things are seemingly going well, and threaten to hurt themselves if you leave. When it comes to sexual coercion and rape, examples include making you feel pressured to perform sexual acts you're uncomfortable with, such as sending nude photos, having sex before you're ready, being pressured to re-enact extreme sex from porn films or being told you don't love them if you say no.

Often the victim in an abusive relationship can never quite put their finger on one thing, but the overwhelming feeling is of a general unease, feeling unsafe, defective, wrong, scared and as if you are going crazy. It's your "yourselfness" that's being consistently undermined, controlled and attacked by the person who claims to love you.

"But he never hit me," is the phrase that comes up repeatedly when talking to teenage victims of emotionally abusive relationships. Another is: "It's my fault. I'm so crazy. I'm the one who's impossible, not him." Or: "Isn't that just what relationships are like?" Yet emotional abuse and coercive control are abuse, even if the perpetrator never physically hurts their victim.

Unfortunately, discussions around abuse are almost as toxic as abuse itself, with society offering very mixed messages about what is and isn't acceptable. Victories in the campaign to seriously tackle psychological violence against women often feel like one step forward and two back. Coercive control became illegal in 2015, but the majority of cases are dropped without charge. The MeToo movement may have empowered many victims to share their stories of sexual violence, but rape conviction rates have plummeted to such lows that it feels as if it has been practically decriminalised.

Popular culture does little to help combat poisonous and confusing messages. In fact, it consistently perpetuates male-on-female abuse as aspirational love stories. Romances currently on Netflix include Noah threatening to kill himself to get a date in The Notebook, Edward repeatedly stalking Bella in Twilight, and even in Friends, "lovable" Ross repeatedly showing excessive jealousy and ownership of Rachel. All of these abusive behaviours are seen as gestures of love, and rewarded with the couple reaching "happily ever after" – rather than the more likely option of the woman suffering long-term psychological trauma. And psychological abuse can be extremely hard to recover from.

All this may make it seem as if tackling relationship abuse is insurmountable, but education is key. That is why Women's Aid has launched the website Love Respect as a vital resource for young people. We are rarely more vulnerable than when we are in love – particularly when we are in love for the first time. Educating young people on abusive behaviours in a relationship isn't "the death of romance" – it's about making everyone realise that abuse was never romantic to begin with.

*3 October 2019*

# Are a third of domestic abuse victims men?

By Grace Rahman

> **'For every three victims of domestic abuse, two will be female, one will be male.' —**
>
> *ManKind Initiative, March 2018*

We've been asked by a reader to look into what percentage of domestic abuse victims are male.

Males made up 31%, or one in every three, of those aged between 16 and 74 who reported having been the victims of domestic abuse since they were 16. That's according to a large survey of crime in England and Wales.

This includes those who've suffered abuse from a partner or family member, and includes non-physical abuse, threats, force, sexual assault or stalking.

## How do we know?

In the year ending March 2018, 29% of women and 13% of men aged 16 to 59 interviewed for the Crime Survey for England and Wales said that they'd experienced some form of domestic abuse since the age of 16.

That's the equivalent of around 2.2 million men and 4.8 million women in the overall population who are estimated to have experienced domestic abuse since the age of 16—so men account for 31% of the estimated total number.

Because of the way this is calculated there is some uncertainty around the exact numbers: there could be around 200,000 more or less than this. The figures also don't tell us how many individual cases of abuse these people have experienced.

This figure includes all types of domestic abuse, including from family members or partners, and physical, sexual and non-physical abuse, as well as stalking. Looking at those individual types of abuse, 29% of those who report being a victim of partner abuse were men. Of those who said they had experienced family abuse, 36% were men.

The Crime Survey has just started asking people aged 60 to 74 whether they have experienced domestic abuse (although the survey is just for households so may miss those in care homes). The prevalence in this group was slightly lower—9% of men and 19% of women in this age group reported that they had experienced domestic abuse since they were 16.

Looking at those percentages among the total population aged 60 to 74 who had experienced domestic abuse around 31% were male and 69% were female.

## Who has experienced abuse?

Percentage of men and women aged 16-59 surveyed who reported having experienced some form of domestic abuse* since they were 16, by type of abuse

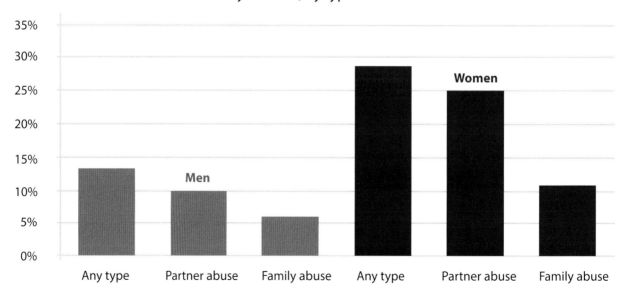

\* This does not include the newer coercive control offence, but does include family, partner, physical sexual and non-physical abuse, and stalking.

Source: ONS, Domestic abuse: findings from the Crime Survey for England and Wales: year ending March 2018

# Prevalence of domestic abuse in the last year

Percentage of adults aged 16-59 in England and Wales surveyed who said they had experienced domestic abuse* in the last year, years ending March 2005 to 2018*

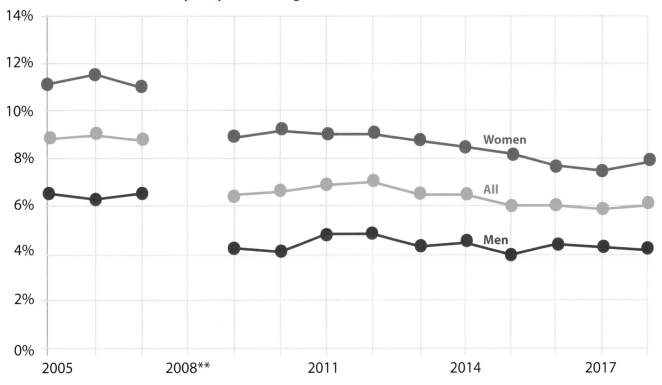

* This does not include the newer coercive control definition of domestic abuse, but does include family, partner, physical sexual and non-physical abuse, and stalking.  ** Data from 2008 is not comparable.

Source: ONS, Domestic abuse: findings from the Crime Survey for England and Wales: year ending March 2018

## How is data on domestic abuse recorded?

The prevalence of domestic abuse is notoriously hard to measure, as it requires victims to report it to the police or surveys. It's also difficult to measure how often it's happening.

The Crime Survey for England and Wales is based on interviews with almost 35,000 people living in households. One of the benefits of this survey is that it picks up crimes that have not been reported to the police.

While a lot of the interview is face-to-face, much of the reporting of domestic abuse which we've looked into here is based on "self-completion", where respondents answer questions using a tablet. The ONS says this "allows respondents to feel more at ease when answering these sensitive questions".

This survey's definition of domestic abuse doesn't include the newer offence of "coercive and controlling behaviour". This is emotional and psychological abuse that doesn't always include physical violence.

### Around 35% of people who have experienced domestic abuse in the last year were men

4% of men and 8% of women aged between 16 and 59 surveyed said they had experienced domestic abuse within the last year. That equates to an estimated 695,000 men and 1.3 million women.

Men make up 35% of the total number of 16 to 59-year-olds who reported they had experienced domestic abuse within the last year.

The ONS says the prevalence of domestic abuse has shown "little change from year to year" and the drop since 2005 is the result of "the cumulative effect of small reductions over time". It says: "This trend has mainly been driven by reductions in partner abuse, which has decreased from a prevalence rate of 5.2% to 4.5% [between 2012 and 2018]."

*7 December 2018*

Of those aged 16-74 who told the Crime Survey for England and Wales that they had experienced some form of domestic abuse since they were 16, a third were male and two thirds were female.

# Male victims of domestic abuse face barriers to accessing support services – new study

An article from The Conversation.

By Eszter Szilassy

THE CONVERSATION

**M**en who experience domestic violence and abuse face significant barriers to getting help and access to specialist support services, our latest study shows.

Although the amount, severity and impact of domestic violence and abuse experienced by women is much higher than that experienced by men, men can also suffer significantly as a result of abuse from a partner, ex-partner or an adult family member.

An earlier study of 1,368 male patients in GP clinic waiting rooms in the UK found that more than one in four had experienced abusive behaviour from a partner or ex-partner. They were also between two and three times more likely to have symptoms of depression and anxiety.

The experiences of many men who are survivors of domestic violence and abuse are similar to those of women. Like female survivors, they find it hard to identify coercion and control as abuse, and to disclose to healthcare professionals that the person who is supposed to love and protect them is harming them. Although they want the abuse to stop and to protect their children from the impact of abuse, they might not necessarily want to end the relationship.

Despite these similarities, the needs of male survivors have been comparatively neglected. Although men also need specialist support, they often face scepticism from healthcare professionals when they disclose this information.

We undertook a review of qualitative studies exploring the barriers to seeking help and the experiences of male victims of domestic violence and abuse in accessing services. Our paper, published in BMJ Open, not only brings together findings not previously reviewed and synthesised, but also provides evidence for developing services to support men who have suffered domestic violence and abuse.

Our findings confirm what has been found in previous studies about barriers men face in seeking help. It has also given us new insights into what hinders and helps professionals and services to provide effective support.

## Reasons for not seeking help

The main reason men don't seek help is a fear of not being believed, embarrassment at talking about the abuse, and the feeling of being "less of a man". Men also worried about the welfare of their partner, damaging their relationship or losing contact with their children if they opened up to someone outside their personal network of family and friends. Others lacked the confidence to seek help as a result of the abuse.

The study also found that men were often not aware of specialist support services or felt they were not appropriate for male survivors of abuse. When men did seek help, they did so usually when their situation had reached a crisis point. While both men and women are reluctant to seek professional help for their abuse, there is an added barrier for men: many fear being falsely accused of being the perpetrator.

Confidentiality was very important to those seeking help from services, as were trust and a non-judgemental attitude. Male survivors raised the importance of the continuity and quality of relationships with professionals to whom they disclose the details. Even if they did not report abuse at the time of a crisis, a positive interaction with a professional influenced their decision to disclose the violence and abuse they experienced at a later date.

There were mixed views about how easy it was to open up to doctors and many men said they preferred to get help from a female professional.

We recommend that services should be more inclusive and tailored more effectively to address the needs of diverse male survivor groups, including those in same-sex relationships. Services should offer ongoing support and be widely advertised. Images and wording of publicity materials for services should represent different types of masculinity and sexuality. Also, health professionals need specialised training to address the specific needs of men and to foster greater levels of trust.

*12 June 2019*

# Gravesham woman lost her home after partner was bailed out for domestic abuse

By Sophie Bird

A Gravesham woman sofa surfed for two years after losing her house while her abuser lived there for free. The woman - who has asked to remain anonymous - was in an abusive relationship for 14 years.

She said: 'I have a masters degree. We had a home fit for Instagram, we had holidays and nice clothes. From the outside we were doing well.

'No one knew I didn't have a door key for my own house and my clothes were picked out for me in the morning.

'No one knew that my phone was monitored via iPad, the mileage on my car was checked, cups were inspected in the cupboard and bins were checked for signs of guests.

'If I decided to give someone a lift home after work, my car would be sold the next day.

'I invited a neighbour in for a cup of tea, the next week the neighbour would be told I had mental health problems and they were brave for spending time with me alone.

'No one knew because there was no shouting or screaming coming from the house.

'I had not made a single decision for myself in over a decade.

'I was brainwashed and thought this was what marriage was.'

Between 2015/16, she tried to leave five times. But she returned each time when her abuser pursued her.

However, in September 2016, two officers came to her door and began to ask about her relationship.

The officers said she was a victim of coercive control and wanted to take her to the station while they arrested her partner.

She begged them on her hands and knees not to do this, explained her partner always gets what they want.

But she was told they were able to arrest her abuser without her consent as it was a domestic abuse case.

The police assured her a statement would be written, her partner would be arrested, then she could go home. Feeling she had no choice, she followed them.

Half an hour after the station called her partner in for questioning, the abuser had taken all the money from the victim's account and reported her phone stolen.

She stayed with her sister on the understanding it was not for the long-term as she was assured she could soon return home.

She was later told her partner was bailed out to their house on the condition they kept a 200 meter distance from her.

She said: 'I told the police this was crazy because I owned the home.'

Later she was told bail terms could not be changed as occupation disputes are a civil matter so she would need to go through the civil court.

With no money, no way to contact anyone and no support services available over the weekend, she was left to find somewhere to stay.

She and her child slept on a relative's sofa for the weekend and on the following week visited the One Stop Shop in Gravesend.

They were supportive and reassuring and directed her to a legal advisor who could help with paperwork to get her house back in court.

However, because she was not in receipt of benefits she was not eligible for free legal support.

She was advised twice to quit her job at the NHS, apply for benefits then apply for legal aid after six to eight weeks.

She said: 'We had what we stood up in and we had nowhere at all to stay for an extended period.

'I couldn't get a crisis loan because I wasn't receiving benefits and the council would not help me with accommodation because I owned a home.'

Many other women fleeing domestic violence in Kent are turned away by their council and told to return to the property where they lived with their abuser as they are technically not homeless.

According to a Gravesham council spokesman, this situation 'would make the person concerned ineligible for social housing due to their ownership or part ownership of a property.

'This does not mean that they would not be eligible for advice to resolve their housing need. Advice given would be specific to each individual's needs.

'It will range from how to secure alternative accommodation, which is likely to be in the private rented sector, to being given advice about agencies they may choose to approach for advice about their safety.'

For almost two weeks the mum-of-one called the police every day to get help collecting her belongings, unable to get another bank account without her ID.

On the 12th day she was told it was not a constructive use of police time and her items were not considered essential because she had gone without them.

She then watched as some of her and her child's belongings were sold on Facebook, which the police could do nothing about as it was a civil matter.

At the end of a month of sofa surfing, she used her pay to apply for an emergency occupation order and went to court months later.

She explained: 'Because my ex was in receipt of benefits they had legal representation.

'I had to go to court by myself and go up against my abuser and a barrister alone.

'The judge stated although the house was in my name, as it was purchased during our marriage it would be classed as joint property and therefore would need to be settled in a divorce, which would take months.'

All the while, her partner was living in her house running up the victim's debt. She was able to take her name off of the utility bills, but not the mortgage or council tax.

So while no one was paying the bills her credit rating dropped and was unable to privately rent.

Her home eventually went up for repossession and there was nothing she could do.

She was also given a county court judgment (CCJ) for not paying council tax.

To make matters worse, her partner was not prosecuted for the domestic abuse because the majority of the evidence was from before the coercive control laws came into force in 2015.

Following this, she went to family court to settle custody of her child. She now has to see her abuser every other week.

After two years of living on sofas or in box rooms, a relative inherited a property from a family bereavement.

They agreed to rent the property out to her, where she now lives with her best friend who she married in the summer.

She believes the system is massively flawed, adding: "Rather than being designed to remove the abuser from your life and assisting you to rebuild, it is designed to strip you of everything.

'It assumes that all domestic abuse happens in low-income relationships and survivors don't work, don't have lives, don't own anything, don't have anything to lose.

'But the truth is it happens to all kinds of families in all kinds of circumstances they can't have these blanket rules.

'For me it was like they asked me to exchange my dignity for freedom.'

*24 February 2020*

# Domestic violence is widely accepted in most developing countries, new study reveals

Societal acceptance of domestic violence against women is widespread in developing countries, with 36 per cent of people believing it is justified in certain situations.

Using Demographic and Health Surveys conducted between 2005-2017, researchers at the University of Bristol analysed data from 1.17 million men and women in 49 low- and middle-income countries.

These findings, published in the journal PLOS ONE (Oct. 31) and funded by the Economic and Social Research Council (ESRC) Future Research Leaders award, will help shape national and international strategies to prevent domestic violence.

Surveys measured whether people thought a husband or partner was justified in beating his wife or partner if she goes out without telling him, argues with him, neglects the children, refuses to have sex or burns the food, or he suspects her of being unfaithful.

On average, 36 per cent of people thought it was justified in at least one of these situations. Attitudes towards domestic violence varied significantly across the 49 countries with only three per cent of people justifying it in the Dominican Republic, in the Caribbean, compared to 83 per cent in Timor-Leste, South East Asia.

Overall, the societal acceptance of domestic violence was higher in South Asia with nearly half the population (47 per cent) justifying it and in Sub-Saharan Africa (38 per cent) compared with Latin America and the Caribbean (12 per cent), Europe and Central Asia (29 per cent).

In 36 of the 49 countries, mainly in South East Asia and Sub-Saharan Africa, women were more likely to justify the behaviour than men.

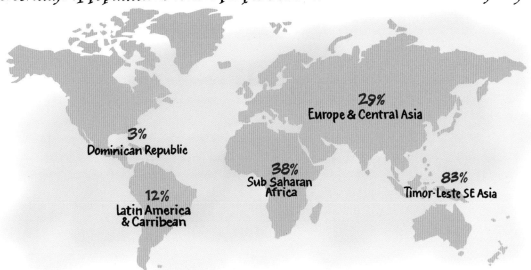

## SOCIETAL ACCEPTANCE
### Percentage of populations where people think domestic violence can be justified

**3%** Dominican Republic

**29%** Europe & Central Asia

**38%** Sub Saharan Africa

**12%** Latin America & Carribean

**83%** Timor-Leste SE Asia

Country-level factors, especially the political environment, played an important role in the acceptance of domestic violence. For example, this attitude of acceptance was more prevalent in countries which have experienced frequent and severe political conflict within the past five years.

Furthermore, the societal acceptance of domestic violence among men was lower in countries with more democratic regimes.

People in countries where women had more economic rights were less likely to justify domestic violence. These findings suggest that expanding women's economic rights can serve to challenge existing social norms around gender roles and the expectations of women and men.

Dr LynnMarie Sardinha, an ESRC Research Fellow in Domestic Violence and Health at the University of Bristol, led the research. She said: "This is the first study of its kind and the insights it gives us into people's attitudes towards domestic violence in the Global South and the influence of country-level factors and environment are invaluable if we're to tackle this global problem.

'The widespread justification of domestic violence by women in highly patriarchal societies suggests women have internalised the idea that a husband who physically punishes his wife or verbally reprimands her has exercised a right that serves her interest. They perceive this behaviour as legitimate disciplining, rather than an act of violence.

'Our findings highlight the need for tailored, geographically-differentiated and gender-specific interventions targeting acceptance of domestic violence. There is need for much greater focus on addressing the acceptance of domestic violence through targeted initiatives in societies affected by political conflict. Although domestic violence is exacerbated during and after armed conflict it's prevention in these societies has received little attention.

'Interestingly, our findings suggest that the commonly-used measures of countries' gender quality scores, for example, women's labour force participation, and number of seats held by women in national parliament, did not significantly influence society's acceptance of domestic violence. This highlights the need for international domestic violence prevention policies to consider that a sole focus on narrowly defined economic or political 'empowerment' alone are not sufficient in challenging existing discriminatory gender norms.

'Given that, as estimated by the World Health Organisation, 30 per cent of women globally have experienced physical or sexual violence from an intimate partner at least once in their lifetime, the prevention of domestic violence is both urgent and vital.

'Domestic violence has serious consequences for women's physical, mental, sexual and reproductive health, negatively impacts on the well-being of children and families and has implications for wider society's economic and social development.'

This project resulted in the construction of a first-of-its-kind global meta-database on societal attitudes to domestic violence, and a comprehensive range of diverse high quality internationally-comparable socio-economic, political and legislative metadata from UN sources and other topic-specific databases.

Researchers hope the findings will inform the development of effective prevention programmes, targeting the factors which lead to domestic violence being accepted by different societies.

Several multilateral organisations, including the World Health Organisation and the United Nations, have already expressed an interest in using the data to help monitor its goal of achieving gender equality and empowering all women and girls (goal five of the UN Sustainable Goals Agenda to achieve a better and more sustainable future for all) that includes the elimination of all forms of violence against women and girls.

*31 October 2018*

# Government publishes landmark domestic abuse bill

The government has unveiled the most comprehensive package ever to tackle domestic abuse.

The landmark draft Domestic Abuse Bill has been published today (Monday 21 January), aimed at supporting victims and their families and pursuing offenders. It comes as it is revealed the estimated cost for domestic abuse victims in the year ending March 2017 in England and Wales was £66 billion.

To help tackle the crime, new legislation will:

◆ introduce the first ever statutory government definition of domestic abuse to specifically include economic abuse and controlling and manipulative non-physical abuse - this will enable everyone, including victims themselves, to understand what constitutes abuse and will encourage more victims to come forward

◆ establish a Domestic Abuse Commissioner to drive the response to domestic abuse issues

◆ introduce new Domestic Abuse Protection Notices and Domestic Abuse Protection Orders to further protect victims and place restrictions on the actions of offenders

◆ prohibit the cross-examination of victims by their abusers in the family courts

◆ provide automatic eligibility for special measures to support more victims to give evidence in the criminal courts

The Home Office has published a report into the economic and social cost of domestic abuse, which reveals the crime for victims in England and Wales cost an estimated £66 billion in the year ending March 2017.

According to the research, the vast majority of this cost (£47 billion) was a result of the physical and emotional harm of domestic abuse, however it also includes other factors such as cost to health services (£2.3 billion), police (£1.3 billion) and victim services (£724 million).

Minister for Crime, Safeguarding and Vulnerability, Victoria Atkins said:

'I have heard absolutely heartbreaking accounts of victims whose lives have been ripped apart because of physical, emotional or economic abuse they have suffered by someone close to them.

The draft Domestic Abuse Bill recognises the complex nature of these horrific crimes and puts the needs of victims and their families at the forefront.

This government is absolutely committed to shining a light on domestic abuse to ensure this hidden crime does not remain in the shadows.'

It is estimated that around two million adults experience domestic abuse each year, affecting almost 6% of all adults. Women are twice as likely to be victims than men.

The draft bill will introduce measures:

◆ to address coercive control and economic abuse, and how domestic abuse affects children

◆ to transform the response in the justice system

The bill will also ban the distressing practice of domestic abuse victims being cross-examined by perpetrators in the family courts.

Between the draft bill and its consultation response, the government is making 120 commitments to tackle domestic abuse. Amongst these are a series of non-legislative measures which include:

◆ £8 million of Home Office funding to support children affected by domestic abuse

◆ a new crisis support system for those with no recourse to public funds

◆ additional funding and capacity building for services for disabled, elderly and LGTB victims

◆ updated support, training and guidance on economic abuse

◆ new and additional training for job centre work coaches, police, social workers and probation staff to help them recognise and effectively tackle abuse

- improved support for victims in the family court
- additional £500,000 funding for provisions for male victims

**Sandra Horley CBE, Chief Executive of Refuge, said:**

'Refuge welcomes the draft bill announced by the government today. Refuge staff deal with the human misery of domestic violence every day. The cost to women and children's lives is devastating. But now the immense cost to the taxpayer has been laid bare, too. Domestic violence is truly everybody's business.

This bill represents a once in a generation opportunity to address domestic violence; but in order to do so, we must ensure its aspirations are matched by adequate resource. We will continue to work closely with the government to ensure the final bill meets the needs of the women and children we support.'

*21 January 2019*

# Enhanced domestic abuse bill introduced to Parliament

Ground-breaking Domestic Abuse Bill to receive First Reading in the House of Commons.

The government has set out an enhanced version of the landmark Domestic Abuse Bill to Parliament, which will go even further to support and protect victims and punish perpetrators.

The bill is the most comprehensive package ever to tackle this horrendous crime and has been widely welcomed by charities and stakeholders.

Following through on the pledge to bring the bill back to Parliament, it includes new measures, such as requiring tier one local authorities (county councils and unitary authorities) in England to provide support and ensure safe accommodation for victims and their children. The bill will also improve on the previous pledge to ban abusers from cross-examining their victims in the family courts, to apply to all family proceedings where there is evidence of domestic abuse.

Domestic Abuse Protection Orders and Protection Notices are powerful tools to protect victims immediately and offer flexible, longer-term protection by imposing requirements on perpetrators. This could include prohibiting contact with the victim or forcing a perpetrator into alcohol or drug treatment programmes.

The government has also announced it will fund any court costs for police applying for these Orders under the pilot, ensuring cost will not be a barrier to police implementing this important tool.

The bill's measures are part of a wider response to tackle crime including recruiting 20,000 additional police officers and offering a record funding settlement to police forces.

**Home Secretary Priti Patel said:**

'An astonishing 2.4 million people in England and Wales have suffered domestic abuse. That is unacceptable, and the reason why it is so important to shine a light on this crime.

The Domestic Abuse Bill is a monumental step to empower victims and survivors, provide protection and tackle perpetrators at the earliest stage.

Through this bill and bolstering law enforcement, we will be able to keep millions of victims safe.'

**Lord Chancellor and Secretary of State for Justice Robert Buckland said:**

'This bill will bolster our response to domestic abuse on every level – strengthening protections for victims, whilst ensuring perpetrators feel the full force of the law.

From giving courts greater powers through new prevention orders, to barring abusers from cross-examining their victim in the family courts, we are delivering a justice system more resilient than ever to the tackle this horrific crime.'

**Minister for Safeguarding Victoria Atkins said:**

'Too many people have to live in fear of abuse – whether it be physical, emotional or economic - from those who should make them feel safe and loved.

This bill will provide support to the victims and survivors of this horrendous crime so that they can go some way to feeling safe again.'

**Sandra Horley CBE, Chief Executive of national domestic abuse charity Refuge, said:**

'Refuge welcomes the re-introduction of the Domestic Abuse Bill, which is significantly enhanced by the addition of a legal duty on local authorities to provide refuge accommodation.

This bill offers the government a real opportunity to transform the response to domestic abuse in this country, but key to its success will be meeting this duty with adequate funding, so that no woman or child is ever turned away when seeking safety.

Refuge will continue to work with the government to strengthen the bill as it progresses into law, and to ensure it best protects the survivors whose very lives depend on it.'

Adina Claire, Acting co chief executive of Women's Aid Federation of England, said:

'With the number of women killed at a 14 year high, the return of the Domestic Abuse Bill to parliament is welcome. Crucially, the legal duty on local authorities could be life-saving, and we will continue to call on the government to deliver a secure funding future for specialist women's services to support this new legal duty.

We are pleased the government has listened to our calls for a wider ban on cross-examination to protect all survivors who face this traumatising practice, but there remains a long way to go before the family courts are truly safe.

We will now work with government and parliament to strengthen the bill to meet the needs of every woman and child experiencing domestic abuse, including migrant women who continue to face dangerous barriers to protection and support.'

The bill has been designed to be future-proof from any new ways perpetrators try to control their victims. It will encompass worrying new trends such as 'tech abuse' – where abusers use personal and home devices and smart gadgets to control their victims. Recent figures from the charity Refuge, whose domestic abuse helpline is funded by the Home Office, show that almost three quarters (72%) of people who spoke to them had been abused through technology.

Economic abuse, which limits access to a victim's fundamental economic resources such as money, food, transport, clothing, utilities, employment and housing, will also be specifically referenced in the definition of domestic abuse to raise awareness of this type of abuse.

Further to these measures, the government has begun a review into what support can be provided to migrant victims of domestic abuse, in addition to looking at what more can done to stop the so called 'rough sex' defence being used by perpetrators in court to attempt to escape justice.

Since the bill was first announced, the government has appointed Nicole Jacobs to be the designate Domestic Abuse Commissioner, who has already begun her important work championing victims and survivors, while constantly monitoring UK legislation to make sure the UK remains a world leader in tackling domestic abuse. This includes looking at what support the government can provide children who have been affected by domestic abuse.

3 March 2020

# Domestic abuse bill not enough to save 'life-saving' services, campaigners warn

'Women and children have nowhere to go so they are staying with their perpetrators or becoming homeless and destitute'.

By Maya Oppenheim, Women's Correspondent

The domestic abuse bill announced by the government does not do enough to tackle cuts to 'life-saving' services which are pushing increasing numbers of domestic abuse victims into homelessness, campaigners have warned.

Boris Johnson's first Queen's Speech since becoming prime minister included a commitment to reintroducing the legislation, which was dropped because of his unlawful suspension of parliament last month.

The domestic abuse bill has been fiercely criticised by campaigners for not counteracting the cuts refuges for domestic abuse victims have endured in recent years.

Andrea Simon, of the End Violence Against Women Coalition, said: 'The bill does not adequately provide for life-saving services for victims of domestic abuse. They need to give them much more money. In many cases, refuges are running on their reserves to keep open.

'It is not a sustainable situation. Failing to sustainably resource the sector puts the lives of women and children at risk. Women are being turned away from refuge services every day and this is putting them in very dangerous and precarious situations. Women and children have nowhere to go so they are staying with their perpetrators or becoming homeless and destitute – this is particularly for migrant women.

'We have seen a huge rise in homelessness for migrant victims of abuse. They can't access housing benefits or refuge space and often can't access private rental options because of immigration checks on private landlords. Specialist services for black and ethnic minority women have experienced the most cuts.'

She noted survivors of abuse and campaigners were promised legislation more than two years ago by a government which promised to 'transform' the response to domestic abuse but concluded they had 'under-delivered'.

Victims in need of a refuge are finding it harder than ever to find a free bed, with 60 per cent unable to find housing, most commonly due to lack of space. One in six refuges have closed since 2010 and local authority spending on refuges has been cut from £31.2m in 2010 to £23.9m in 2017. Ms Simon also criticised the bill for failing to protect migrant women – explaining the government had proposed a review of migrant victims of domestic abuse to inform changes to the legislation in the wake of criticism.

She added: 'However, this review has felt particularly rushed, has lacked transparency and limited engagement with specialist organisations that work with migrant women.'

Gisela Valle, of the Latin American Women's Rights Service, also hit out at the domestic abuse bill for excluding migrant women.

She said: 'This legislation has been billed as a once-in-a-generation opportunity to address domestic abuse, but it ignores one of those most vulnerable groups. It is very worrying. We are calling for the government to change this.

'Migrant status is being used as a way of coercing and controlling women who are experiencing domestic abuse. It traps women in abusive situations for longer. Our research found migrant women stay for an average of five years before trying to access any kind of support.

'The abusers tell them if they report the abuse, they will be arrested, detained or deported. If you go to the police as a migrant woman, in some cases you actually get detained right then and there and then you could be deported depending on the situation. The police share information with the Home Office.'

Ms Valle said it was 'paradoxical' that the bill is meant to be the instrument which ratifies the Istanbul Convention – a pan-European convention tackling violence against women – when it directly contravenes it.

The Istanbul Convention states women who experience violence should not be discriminated against on the basis of their immigration status.

David Cameron, the former prime minister, signed the convention in 2012 but it has still not been ratified – meaning it is currently in limbo and the UK is not legally bound to follow it. Britain is one of the last EU members – along with Bulgaria, Hungary and a handful of others – to ratify it.

Karla McLaren, of Amnesty International, said: 'The bill will fail unless it ensures all survivors – regardless of immigration status – are offered safety and protection.'

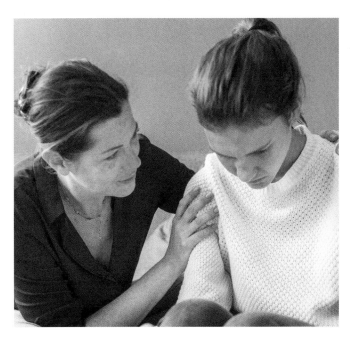

Refuge, the largest provider of specialist domestic violence services in the UK, has argued the bill falls short in a number of areas.

The organisation has called for the legislation to overhaul the single payment structure of Universal Credit – arguing it 'facilitates and exacerbates abuse by potentially handing over control of the household's entire income overnight'.

The domestic abuse bill introduces the first ever statutory definition of domestic abuse to include economic abuse and controlling and manipulative behaviour that is not physical – as well as including measures which mean perpetrators will no longer be able to directly cross-examine victims in family courts.

The legislation introduces new Domestic Abuse Protection Notices and Domestic Abuse Protection Orders to further safeguard victims and also includes provisions to place a legal duty on councils to offer secure homes for those fleeing violence and their children.

A spokesperson for the Home Office said: 'We are committed to ensuring that all victims of domestic abuse receive the support they need and the domestic abuse bill is a once in a generation opportunity to ensure that this is provided.

'The bill will include a new legal duty for local authorities to provide essential, life-saving support services in safe accommodation for survivors of domestic abuse and their children.

'We are also aware of the concerns around the support available to migrant victims of domestic abuse. In May, we hosted a roundtable to discuss this issue further and we are currently carrying out a review into the Government's overall response to migrant victims of domestic abuse.'

*14 October 2019*

# How to prevent abuse in teenage relationships

An article from The Conversation.

Nicola Bowes Forensic Psychologist and Senior Lecturer in Forensic Psychology, Cardiff Metropolitan University and Karen De Claire Senior Lecturer in Forensic Psychology, Cardiff Metropolitan University

THE CONVERSATION

The UK has made some positive shifts in legislating against intimate partner violence among adults in recent years. However, physical, psychological and sexual violence in teenage relationships is still a very real problem.

A recent study of young people – aged 15 to 18-years -old – in relationships in the UK and Spain, found that 21% experience serious victimisation by partners (an example given was one partner slamming the other into a wall). A further 30.1% meanwhile are subject to mild aggression including pushing, grabbing or shoving.

Across Europe there are similar findings. 42% of young women and 39% of young men (aged 16 to 17-years-old) experience physical violence. And a Portuguese study has revealed that 31% of girls age 15 to 16-years-old experience sexual violence in relationships.

Psychological victimisation – including hostile attitudes, intimidation or restrictive control – is the most prevalent type of relationship violence that young people (aged 14-20) experience. Some studies report rates as high as 94% of girls and 93% of boys.

## Ending the violence

Having positive peer relationships during adolescence has been shown to be one of the most important things for teenagers' well being, health, school attendance and achievement, and self-esteem. Lack of peer relationships, loneliness, or negative peer relationships have a hugely negative affect on those same things.

Our teenage years are when we develop the skills we need to form, maintain and enjoy healthy relationships. Adolescence is a time to fall in love, to have our hearts broken and learn how to mend them again. It's the time when our peer group is most important to us. We rely on them to help us through that roller coaster journey and we support our friends as they ride the same.

But if that journey is marked by violence, it can potentially take years for the victim to recover from what they have experienced. So how can we get teenagers to see that either acting violent or suffering under it is a problem?

Some researchers have suggested a focus on changing attitudes to things like traditional gender-related roles and myths about them – for example, that women can't do certain jobs or roles at work or home – but it has not been proved that addressing these issues might reduce violence in young people's relationships.

## Light ahead

We are working on a project that takes a new approach to teenage relationship violence. Rather than simply educating or trying to change attitudes, our method draws on the assets that young people already have, to help them identify their own problems and develop their relationship skills.

One review of the research suggested that school projects are more successful at preventing violence in relationships when they involve participation (using drama). That is as well as addressing factors such as gender equality, healthy relationships and non-violent conflict resolution. It has also been suggested that specific training for young people to improve skills such as communication, negotiation and conflict resolution may also be helpful.

So our EU-funded project puts these ideas into practice. We are working with teenagers aged between 13 and 15 at schools in six European countries (Italy, Spain, Portugal, Romania, Poland, UK). Our aim is to help them identify, share and strengthen their positive assets and relationship skills by using drama, film and peer learning.

Many projects in the area of teenage dating violence focus on deficits and risk factors – such as trauma or a disadvantaged family life – that may be implicated in the violence. But Lights 4 Violence uses a different approach, focusing on individual strengths such as assertiveness, pro-social problem solving, as well as the attributes individuals can rely on within their families, peer groups and school.

The teenagers will learn about communicating their feelings, recognising the feelings of others – and develop assertiveness skills to address and resolve conflict in their relationships. In addition, teachers will be equipped with the skills to help the young people empower and protect themselves from abusive relationships.

It is hugely important that schools are not only supported in stopping teenage relationship violence, but also given the right methods to do it – and that is why we are taking this new approach. Simply talking to teens won't work – and we hope that our project will prepare the young people participating to engage in and enjoy positive, healthy relationships.

*9 February 2018*

# Relationship education could help reduce domestic violence

Sarah Page Senior Lecturer, Sociology and Criminology, Staffordshire University and Em Temple-Malt Senior Lecturer, Sociology and Criminology, Staffordshire University

As part of the new-style sex education curriculum, school pupils will soon start learning about healthy intimate relationships – which could help to significantly reduce future domestic abuse in the UK. In recent research we did on this issue we spoke to various professionals who work with victims of domestic abuse. One of them told us that they believe healthy relationships education needs to be 'taught in schools from a young age':

> 'I think kids should know that 'this is what we do', and that 'this isn't what we do'…and it isn't just the basics of you don't hit girls.'
>
> — *The Conversation*

From September 2020, new mandatory regulations will be in force in England and Wales to ensure education includes teaching 'all young people how to stay safe' through the promotion of healthy relationships. All state primary schools will need to provide relationship education, and all secondary schools will provide relationship and sex education.

But independent schools and academies will not have to meet the new requirement. Parents can also opt for their children not to participate in the relationship education sessions. There is also a question around how the new curriculum will be implemented outside of mainstream education – which could include children in care.

## What relationship education should look like

Preventative education on how to recognise abusive and unhealthy relationships is likely to be more cost-effective than services that deal with the aftermath of victims, or the rehabilitation of perpetrators. Educating children about healthy relationships before the age of ten is vital because after this point, attitudes and behaviours become crystallised and resistant to change.

Healthy relationships education needs to ensure that content is modernised to include topics such as coercive control, sexting, cyber-bullying, and online safety. The lessons also need to support younger learners to develop communication and conflict management skills – as well as challenging deeply rooted sexist values in society.

Relationships education should also provide children and young people with both the knowledge and skills to keep calm during initial disagreements. It should also help them to understand how to manage frustration, and avoid behaviours that escalate the argument and lead to violence.

As part of our research, we also interviewed a professional who works with perpetrators of domestic abuse in the criminal justice system. They told us that a 'significant percentage' of perpetrators 'don't understand what a healthy relationship actually is, so then they haven't got the skills to have one.'

We hope that sexist assumptions in relationships, which underpin attitudes to domestic abuse, can be addressed as the new curriculum comes into force. Such education needs to be ongoing and not treated as a one off for there to be a change in attitudes and behaviour.

## Questions over delivery

Research illustrates the effectiveness of teaching younger learners about healthy relationships and advocates that domestic abuse prevention education should become mandatory. Developing educational toolkits for teaching healthy relationships out of research findings is good practice.

Within academia and among those who are trying to stop domestic abuse, there are ongoing debates about who should be delivering domestic abuse prevention education in schools. Should it be teachers or domestic abuse experts?

As part of our research, we also spoke to professionals who work for services that provide domestic abuse prevention education. They told us how it can be hard to get into schools to deliver sessions relating to domestic abuse. So our hope is that the new legislation can help to make easier access into schools for community and voluntary sector organisations equipped to educate around this issue.

But due to funding cuts to voluntary sector organisations – including those that work to combat domestic abuse – there are fears this may not happen. This means that education sessions are likely to be led by teachers within the school – who may not yet be equipped with up-to-date information.

Schools should also be provided with adequate resources to deliver counselling services to address any issues raised through these sessions. Children need support to process their experiences of domestic abuse and any associated trauma. The same is true, in cases where relationship education leads young people to identify unhealthy behaviours in their own and others' intimate relationships.

These are just a few practical considerations to ensure the government achieves its mandate for 'all' young people to get access to life saving relationship education information. About two women are killed by their partner or former partner each week in England and Wales. Effective healthy relationships education is imperative if there is to be a reduction in this figure.

*24 August 2018*

# Worried about a friend?

By Sophie J

**B**eing a good friend is tough at the best of times, right? But trying to be there can be extra hard sometimes, especially if it feels like they're being distant recently. Maybe they're seeing someone new and something's just different about them. Maybe they've started to change how they dress. Maybe they're not around as much – and maybe when you do see them, they're quieter and more distracted.

If you're concerned that your friend could be spending time with someone who doesn't treat them well, then here are some suggestions to help them. Remember, you're not on your own – if you feel overwhelmed, worried or like your friend may be in danger, you can speak to Women's Aid.

### 1. Start by observing – what are the differences in your friend's behaviour?

Does their phone buzz constantly? Do they seem afraid to wear certain outfits or to talk to certain people, when that wasn't the case before? There's a lot we can pick up on just from watching and listening, particularly with someone we know really well.

### 2. Text them to check in, ask them to hang out – make sure they know you're there for them.

It can be tempting to rush in, all guns blazing. But too intense an approach can be overwhelming. All you need to do is keep reinforcing that you are a loyal, non-judgemental mate who isn't going anywhere. Text them to check in. Ask them to hang out at the weekend. Remind them that you're always around for chats.

### 3. Try to avoid any accusatory conversations with them – it may push them away.

I get it: sometimes you just want to march up to your friend and be like 'WHAT IS GOING ON? WHY ARE YOU BEING LIKE THIS?!' But that kind of approach can come across as harsh or disapproving, rather than honest or caring.

Abusers often isolate their boyfriend or girlfriend from loved ones. My own abuser used to tell me that my friends hated me, and that my mum was controlling. Every time anyone raised concerns about the relationship with me, we'd end up arguing – then, when I told my boyfriend about it, he'd say, 'I told you so!' and I'd think, 'Yeah, you were right.' By the time we broke up, I had almost no one.

### 4. But don't forget to share your opinion – they need to know when things are NOT okay.

When I brought up concerns about my relationship with some friends they raised their eyebrows, but never said, 'Wow, that's awful!'

When I broke up with my boyfriend, they told me, 'We're so glad you're not with him – we always hated him but didn't know what to say.' I was shocked. Confiding in them about my abuse was my way of asking, 'Is this okay?'

It wasn't their fault, and they were just trying to be polite. But if your friend confides in you or you see some unacceptable behaviour from their abuser, say, "This is not okay. What can I do to help?"

## 5. Give them a chance to talk – don't pounce on them or talk over them.

My friends asked me to meet up with them in Pizza Hut – with me alone on one side of the table, as if I was interviewing for a job – and said, 'What is going on with you? We want our old friend back.' They kept using the word 'we' and it made me feel like they'd been talking behind my back and judging me. To be grilled in front of all of them felt horrible.

I left as quickly as I could and ran straight to my boyfriend's house, saying, 'You were right about them! They're so mean!' My friends had meant well. But their approach actually pushed me closer to my boyfriend. Giving your friend a chance to tell you their side of things can help a lot. Remember, they're most likely dealing with someone who's quite controlling and demanding, so they're probably feeling really stressed and tense.

Top tips to have those difficult conversations:

**Believe them:** Remember, it's not up to you to decide whether your friend is telling you the truth. You just need to listen and believe what they're saying. Talking about abuse can be very difficult.

**Be supportive:** You might say, 'I'm glad you told me about this. Thanks for trusting me.'

**Don't judge or criticise:** Saying things like, 'How can you put up with this?' won't help your friend. Just thank them for trusting you enough to talk to them. Also, don't criticise the abuser – remember, it's more than likely going to be someone they care about and love.

**Be honest:** Don't be afraid to tell your friend that you're worried about them, that you think they may need help and that maybe they should tell someone else about what's going on.

'It's not your fault': Tell your friend that they're not to blame and they're not responsible for what's happening.

Express your concern: It's up to your friend to decide whether to tell another adult or not. But it's OK for YOU to tell someone if you're really worried that your friend might get hurt. But be honest about this – tell them who you're going to talk to so they don't feel you're sneaking around behind their back.

Thank your friend for trusting you and let them know how strong they are – talking about violence and abuse takes a lot of strength and courage.

## 6. Don't take things personally – this isn't about you.

One of the saddest moments for me was when my friend sent me an email telling me how hurt she was that I hadn't showed up to her 18th birthday party. But I couldn't bring myself to tell her the truth – I was choosing the scenario that would land me in the least amount of 'trouble' with my abuser. Please don't take things personally – I know it's hard not to, but your friend is in a very stressful and potentially scary situation right now.

*January 2020*

# 'Domestic violence prevention course was no cure, but a salvation'

A once-abusive husband defends a programme he says made him rethink his attitude to his wife.

By Jamie Grierson, Home Affairs Correspondent

Gareth Jones once held his wife against a wall with her feet off the ground and screamed at her. For years, he abused Bronwyn, his wife of 15 years, and was twice convicted of offences linked to violent outbursts against her.

But Gareth, 46, is still with Bronwyn. He describes his relationship with her as 'wonderful' and she says she is looking forward to the future.

The optimism is a result of Gareth spending two and a half years voluntarily attending a domestic violence prevention programme. 'It was my salvation,' he says.

'I walked in there thinking it would be some sort of back-slapping exercise, but it wasn't. It completely turned my world upside down.'

Bronwyn says the programme gave Gareth the tools he needs to cope with the issues behind his devastating behaviour. 'The programme was about changing core beliefs of how they perceive women, or perceive their role within a family,' she says. 'Or in life. It literally rocks you to the core.'

On Tuesday, probation inspectors expressed concern that the number of perpetrators being referred to the only course to be accredited by a public authority, Building Better Relationships, was falling, as was the completion rate.

Violence prevention programmes are hugely controversial. This was recently underlined by fierce reaction to a social media campaign by Essex police and county council that many accused of encouraging survivors to stay with perpetrators.

Campaigners and charities cautiously welcome schemes that are appropriately accredited, but said they are concerned they could be used as quicker, cheaper solutions at the expense of safe and effective practices, such as providing refuge to women fleeing abuse. Refuge, the domestic violence charity, has previously said there was a lack of evidence the programmes worked and questioned funding support for "violent men".

But research into the impact of such programmes has produced broadly supportive findings.

Cambridge University researchers found that a two-session counselling programme for low-level, first time domestic abusers cut re-offending rates by a third, while an earlier groundbreaking study, Project Mirabal, led by professors from Durham and London Metropolitan universities, found far fewer women reported being physically injured after their partner had attended a programme, with 61% before compared to 2% after.

Gareth, who lives in North Wales, said he always had a temper but his behaviour spiralled shortly after the death of his 14-month-old daughter.

'I was a very arrogant person,' he says. 'I always saw everyone else's problem as their problem, not my problem. But I was living a lie.'

He first physically assaulted his wife, who at eight stone was half his size, about six years ago. She had just come off a Skype call with her parents, in which he wrongly thought she had said something derogatory about him.

'I just basically exploded. It was awful,' he says. 'I pushed her with such force she went over the double bed and over the other side.'

He was charged and convicted of common assault but after moving out of the home for about six months returned to the family to find nothing had changed. 'The arguments were getting worse and getting physical,' he says.

Bronwyn, 47, a nurse, recalls how Gareth's behaviour deteriorated after he lost their child. 'I've been pushed to the floor and he has stood over me and spat at me when he's been drunk,' she says. 'It's been as bad as that.'

About three years ago, estranged from his wife, Gareth started attending Choose2Change, the violence prevention programme run by the relationship counselling organisation Relate Cymru and accredited by the domestic violence charity Respect.

Based in a North Wales community centre, the meetings are similar to those of Alcoholics Anonymous. Men who have been abusive in variety of ways, physical and emotional, get together under supervision, discuss their experiences and use a variety of interactive exercises to help them understand the impact of their behaviour.

'The reason I changed was listening to other men in my position, realising it's not everyone else around you – it's you,' Gareth says. 'You're the reason everyone is suffering here.'

Bronwyn was astounded by the change in her husband. 'He went on the programme and it's like being with the man I met again,' she says.

The courses require attendees to remain for a minimum of six months and are voluntary. Gareth admits he signed up with a degree of cynicism and arrogance.

'Initially, I was going through the motions,' he says. 'I went with the "well it will look good in court" type of attitude.'

But after two to three months, the programme started to have a life-changing impact and he continued to attend. About 12 months after he started the programme, Gareth moved back home with his wife.

He last attended a session four months ago and now talks about his marriage with enthusiasm and pride. 'It's wonderful, wonderful,' he says. 'We talk – there are no barriers there. One thing it has improved more than anything is communication in the relationship.'

Gareth now works as an advocate for Choose2Change at fundraisers, sharing his experience with others, and calls for

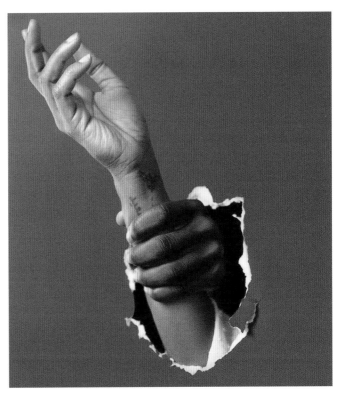

violence prevention programmes to be offered as soon as a perpetrator is identified. 'The programmes are not funded enough or publicised enough,' he says.

'When I was in the jail cells, they were my lowest moments. At that point to have people who've been through it, have an ex-perpetrator come in and say: "This isn't the way, talk to me." If someone had done that to me, I would have been all over it.'

Research has shown that the majority of recorded male perpetrators (83% in one study) had at least two incidents of recorded abuse to their name and, on average, two women a week are killed by a partner or ex-partner in England and Wales.

Provision of safe spaces for women – 1.2 million of whom experienced domestic abuse in the last year, according to official estimates – remains a priority for charities and campaigners.

With funding for refuges under threat, as the government proposes to cut their only guaranteed source of income, Katie Ghose of Women's Aid cautioned that programmes like the one Gareth attended must never be seen as a substitute for real support for victims.

'Perpetrator programmes must be Respect-accredited and must also be underpinned by a national network of specialist domestic abuse services for survivors,' she said. 'If we fail to give the necessary support to survivors, women's lives will continue to be at risk.'

Gareth and Bronwyn agreed for his name to be changed for this piece to protect his identity.

*24 September 2018*

# Key Facts

- Domestic violence is the abuse of one partner within an intimate or family relationship. (page 1)

- Domestic abuse can be physical, emotional, psychological, financial or sexual. (page 1)

- Approximately 90% of those who are raped know the perpetrator prior to the offence. (page 1)

- Analysis of Merseyside Police domestic abuse data found that 95% of coercive control victims were women and 74% of perpetrators were men. (page 2)

- One study found that 95 out of 100 domestic abuse survivors reported experiencing coercive control (Kelly et al, 2014). (page 2)

- There were 17,616 offences of coercive control recorded by the police in the year ending March 2019, compared with 9,053 in the year ending March 2018. (page 3)

- It was not until 2015 that coercive control was officially criminalised in law and recognised as a form of domestic abuse. (page 3)

- In the year ending March 2019, an estimated 2.4 million adults aged 16 to 74 years experienced domestic abuse in the last year (1.6 million women and 786,000 men). (page 4)

- 4.2% of men and 8.4% of women aged 16 to 59 years had experienced domestic abuse within the last year in the year ending March 2019. (page 4)

- 60,641 incidents of domestic abuse were recorded by police in Scotland in 2018-19. (page 7)

- An estimated 90% of children whose mothers are abused witness the abuse. (page 9)

- Two women a week are murdered by a current or ex-partner in England and Wales alone. (page 10)

- False allegations about domestic abuse are extremely rare. (page 11)

- In 2018-2019 there were 2,426 cases of rape and attempted rape reported to Police Scotland. (page 12)

- One in ten women in Scotland has experienced rape & one in five women in Scotland has had someone try to make them have sex against their will. (page 12)

- Research indicates that only 58% of people in Scotland believe that a woman who wears revealing clothing on a night out is 'not at all to blame' for being raped, with 60% saying the same of a woman who is very drunk. (page 12)

- An estimated 1.6 million women aged 16 to 74 years experienced domestic abuse in the year ending March 2019. (page 13)

- The latest figures, which use data from the Crime Survey for England and Wales, found 84 per cent of all victims killed by a partner or former partner are female. The suspect was male in all but two cases. (page 14)

- Female perpetrators now account for 28 per cent of cases - compared to 19 per cent a decade ago. Male perpetrators were still identified in the majority of domestic violence incidents. (page 16)

- Nearly 700 children are identified as being at risk of domestic violence every day, according to analysis of new research by Action for Children. (page 18)

- The Crime Survey estimates that in 2017/18 152,000 people aged 60 to 74 were victims of partner abuse and 66,000 were victims of family abuse. (page 19)

- Around 35% of people who have experienced domestic abuse in the last year were men. (page 25)

- On average, 36 per cent of people in developing countries believe domestic violence is justified in certain situations. (page 28)

- The World Health Organization estimates 30 per cent of women globally have experienced physical or sexual violence from an intimate partner at least once in their lifetime. (page 29)

- 60 per cent of domestic violence victims are unable to find housing, most commonly due to lack of space. One in six refuges have closed since 2010 and local authority spending on refuges has been cut from £31.2m in 2010 to £23.9m in 2017. (page 33)

- A recent study of young people – aged 15 to 18 years old – in relationships in the UK and Spain, found that 21% experience serious victimisation by partners (an example given was one partner slamming the other into a wall). A further 30.1% meanwhile are subject to mild aggression including pushing, grabbing or shoving. (page 34)

- Psychological victimisation – including hostile attitudes, intimidation or restrictive control – is the most prevalent type of relationship violence that young people (aged 14-20) experience. Some studies report rates as high as 94% of girls and 93% of boys. (page 34)

# Glossary

## Clare's Law

Also known as the Domestic Violence Disclosure Scheme, Clare's Law allows people to find out whether someone has a record of abusive offences, or if there is any other information that indicates they may be at risk.

## Coercive control

The term coercive control refers to the aspects of domestic violence that encompass more than just physical abuse, e.g. psychological behaviour that removes a victim's freedom.

## Domestic abuse/violence

Any incident of physical, sexual, emotional or financial abuse that takes place within an intimate partner relationship. Domestic abuse can be perpetrated by a spouse, partner or other family member and occurs regardless of gender, sex, race, class or religion.

## Elder abuse

Physical, emotional or sexual harm inflicted upon an elderly adult. Elder abuse also includes their financial exploitation or neglect of their welfare by people who are directly responsible for their care.

## Emotional abuse

Emotional abuse refers to a victim being verbally attacked, criticised and put down. Following frequent exposure to this abuse, the victim's mental wellbeing suffers as their self-esteem is destroyed and the perpetrator's control over them increases. They may suffer feelings of worthlessness, believing that they deserve the abuse or that if they were to leave the abuser they would never find another partner. A victim may also have been convinced by their abuser that the abuse is their fault. The abuser can use these feelings to manipulate the victim.

## Domestic Abuse Bill

The Domestic Abuse Bill was first announced in 2019. An enhanced draft of the bill was introduced in parliament in March 2020. The bill aims to improve the effectiveness of the justice system in providing protection for victims of domestic abuse and bringing perpetrators to justice and also to strengthen the support for victims of abuse by statutory agencies.

## Financial abuse

Financial, or economic, abuse involves controlling the victim's finances. This limits the victim's independence and ability to access help, and restricts their ability to leave the abusive relationship. Financial abuse can include witholding money or credit cards, exploiting mutual assets and forcing someone to quit their job or work against their will.

## Gaslighting

Psychologically manipulating someone by making them believe their behaviour is their fault.

## Perpetrator programme

A rehabilitation programme for perpetrators of domestic abuse which aims to help them understand and try to change their abusive behaviour.

## Physical abuse

Physical abuse involves the use of violence or force against a victim and can including hitting, slapping, kicking, pushing, strangling or other forms of violence. Physical assault is a crime and the police have the power to protect victims, but in a domestic violence situation it can sometimes take a long time for the violence to come to light. Some victims are too afraid to go to the police, believe they can reform the abuser (who they may still love) or have normalised their abusive situation and do not realise they can get help.

## Refuge

A shelter or safe house, offering a safe place for victims of domestic violence and their children to stay. Refuges can provide practical advice as well as emotional support for victims of domestic abuse until they can find somewhere more permanent to stay.

## Sexual abuse

Sexual abuse occurs when a victim is forced into a sexual act against their will, through violence or intimidation. This can include rape. Sexual abuse is always a crime, no matter what the relationship between the victim and perpetrator.

## Stalking

Repeatedly following, watching or harassing someone. Stalking usually takes place over a long period of time and is made up of lots of different actions, some of which may seem harmless but which can prove extremely distressing to the victim.

# Activities

## Brainstorming

♦ In small groups, discuss what you know about domestic violence. Consider the following:

  • As well as physical violence, what other forms of abuse are types of domestic violence ?

  • What does the term 'coercive control' mean?

  • Who are the victims of domestic abuse?

  • Who are the perpetrators of domestic abuse?

  • What are the common myths surrounding the causes of domestic violence?

## Research

♦ Do some research online looking for cases of domestic violence that have made the news in the UK or globally over the last six months. Select two or three cases, make notes on any striking similarities or differences between them and share your findings with the rest of the class.

♦ What is Clare's Law? Do some research making notes about what the law entails and how it was given its name.

♦ Looking online and referring to the articles in this book on page 8 and pages 30-33, do some further research about the recently introduced Domestic Abuse Bill. What provisions and actions have been proposed to support victims and tackle the issue of domestic violence in the UK? Make notes then discuss what you have found out in small groups.

♦ Create a questionnaire to find out how many people in your class are aware that domestic abuse can happen after a relationship has ended. Draw a graph to illustrate the results.

♦ The 2020 coronavirus pandemic and resulting lockdown has seen an increase in calls to domestic violence helplines. Doing your own research into statistics, can you identify any other events or circumstances that often result in a surge of domestic violence incidents? What have you found?

## Design

♦ Choose one of the articles in this book and create an illustration to highlight the key themes in the article.

♦ Read the article *Challenging the myths* on page 9. In small groups design a campaign of posters illustrating five of the 16 'myths versus reality' facts presented in the piece.

♦ Design a poster or leaflet aimed at helping teenagers to recognise signs of abusive behaviour in their own relationships or those of their friends or family members. Try to illustrate where the boundary lies between someone being nice and someone being controlling and abusive.

♦ Design a poster offering advice for people who are thinking of leaving their abusive partner. Include a list of resources and charities people can go to for information and support. Where would be an ideal place to display it?

## Oral

♦ Your friend tells you that their boyfriend/girlfriend is being emotionally abusive. In pairs, role play a situation in which you ask about this behaviour and give advice.

♦ A third of domestic abuse victims are men. As a class, discuss why you think male victims of domestic violence are less likely to come forward to talk about or report their abuse.

♦ In small groups, discuss the reasons why victims choose to stay with abusive partners.

♦ Think about the article on page 38, *'Domestic violence prevention course was no cure, but a salvation'*. As a class, discuss rehabilitation programmes for domestic violence perpetrators, what they entail and if you think they work.

## Reading/Writing

♦ Choose one of the articles in this book and write a one-paragraph summary. Pick five key points and list them.

♦ Write a short definition of:

  • Coercive control

  • Gaslighting

  • Safeguarding

♦ Watch the film *A Star is Born* starring Lady Gaga and Bradley Cooper. Write a review focussing on the relationship dynamic between the characters Ally and Jackson. Do you think their romance is healthy or unhealthy? Give reasons for your answer.

♦ Write a 500 word diary entry from the point of view of a parent who is suffering domestic violence at the hands of their child.

A

abuse

emotional 1, 41

financial 1, 41

physical 41

sexual 1, 41

*see also* domestic abuse

abuser programmes 38–39, 41

Age UK 19

C

Challen, Sally 3

children

impacts of domestic abuse 9–10

at risk of domestic violence 18

Clare's Law 41

coercive control 2–3, 19, 41

controlling behaviour 2

COVID-19 pandemic, impact of lockdown 17

Crime Survey for England and Wales (CSEW) 25

on domestic abuse 4

on elderly abuse 19

Crown Prosecution Service (CPS), on coercive control 2–3

culture, and domestic abuse 28–29

D

dating violence 20–22

domestic abuse

attitudes towards 28–29

coercive control 2–3, 19, 41

dating violence 20–22

definition 41

elderly people 19

female perpetrators 16

and homelessness 27–28, 32–33

impact of lockdown 17

impact on children 9–10, 18

increase in 13–14

legislation 8, 18, 30–33

men as victims of 10–11, 16, 24–26

myths 9–11

prevention 38–39

in Scotland 6–7, 12

signs of 36–37

societal acceptance of 28–29

statistics 3–5, 24–25

teenagers 20–23, 34–36

and violence 9–10

Domestic Abuse Bill 8, 18, 30–33, 41

E

elder abuse 19, 41

emotional abuse 1, 41

F

femicide 15

Femicide Census 2018 15

financial abuse 1, 41

G

gaslighting 41

gender inequality 13

H

homelessness, and domestic abuse 27–28, 32–33

homicides

domestic 3, 15

*see also* femicide

I

inequality 12–13

M

men, as victims of domestic abuse 10–11, 16, 24–26

N

NSPCC 18

O

Office for National Statistics

       on coercive control 3

       on domestic abuse 4, 24–25


P

perpetrator programmes 38–39, 41

Phillips, Jess 8

physical abuse 41

pornography 10

psychological abuse 1


R

rape 12

Refuge 14

refuges 32–33, 41

       *see also* homelessness

relationship education 35–36


S

Scotland

       domestic abuse 6–7, 12–13

       gender inequality 13

sexual abuse 1, 41

sexual offences 12, 24

stalking 5, 9, 15, 20–21, 24, 41

suicide, threats of 21–22

T

teenagers

       abusive relationships 22–23, 34–36

       dating violence 20–22


V

violence 9–10, 12

violence against women and girls (VAWG) 12–13


W

Women's Aid 3, 14

# Acknowledgements

The publisher is grateful for permission to reproduce the material in this book. While every care has been taken to trace and acknowledge copyright, the publisher tenders its apology for any accidental infringement or where copyright has proved untraceable. The publisher would be pleased to come to a suitable arrangement in any such case with the rightful owner.

The material reproduced in *ISSUES* books is provided as an educational resource only. The views, opinions and information contained within reprinted material in *ISSUES* books do not necessarily represent those of Independence Educational Publishers and its employees.

## Images

Cover image courtesy of iStock. All other images courtesy of Pixabay, Rawpixel and Unsplash.

## Icons

Icons on page 7 were made by freepix from www.flaticon. com.

## Illustrations

Don Hatcher: pages 9 & 29. Simon Kneebone: pages 12 & 37. Angelo Madrid: pages 1 & 19.

## Additional acknowledgements

With thanks to the Independence team: Shelley Baldry, Danielle Lobban, Jackie Staines and Jan Sunderland.

Tracy Biram

Cambridge, May 2020